INTRODUCTION

Murals today range in size from a few square feet to hundreds of square metres and in intention and style they cover the compass of artistic endeavour. With the great watershed and dispersal of all the world's styles through the medium of books and magazines every style has become available. Painted inside small private houses or outside great public buildings they range from abstract romantic to utopian didactic, from photo-realist trompe-d'oeil to anarcho-dadaist naive style, and while some exponents are eagerly exploring the latest methods and materials, many

continue to employ the oldest traditional systems. While some muralists challenge society and are threatened with the most destructive opposition, others are content to reinforce its ancient verities. What distinguishes the mural from the portable painting is its adhesion to a particular wall in a special location. The personality of the wall and the character of the environment, inside or out, are the challenging forces with which muralists of all persuasions and of every period engage!

It must be apparent to everyone that the British Inner City scenery is blighted, demanding renewal and visual stimulation, not only of its decaying nineteenth century

bu
uti
ar
un
pa
opportunity for muralists.

In writing what follows we are setting out to establish a guide to enable artists, groups or communities to find, set up, and carry out mural projects. We do not intend to fix on any particular method, but want to suggest opportunities, techniques and processes, and ways of dealing with special problems, not hiding our own bias, but making the information so catholic it will be of use to all.

Lion hunt relief from Nineveh, Assyria, 645 BC.

History

People all over the world produce murals and have done so for centuries, and from the photographs, books and postcards now available it is obvious that there are countless traditions of the use of murals representing a wide range of themes and techniques on a variety of walls and other surfaces.

Images from non-Western cultures, generate new ideas and show a limitless potential for the development of murals in the future. They also put recent European art into perspective, explode the myth of Greece as the sole womb of culture, and challenge the concept of art as a linear progression and development through history. The oil painting tradition becomes a

mere hiccup in the history of art and, since the activities of muralists in these other countries were collective and social, the whole notion of the artist as an isolated individual seems fragile.

Britain has a long history of mural painting. Interiors of churches in medieval times were elaborately painted with images and decorations in strong colours. Traces of these can be seen, for example in Canterbury Cathedral, Durham and Winchester. Far from being grey and cold they were gaudy, visually thrilling, and full of didactic imagery.

The advent of both Protestantism and the wealthy private patron who wanted rectilinear portable paintings resulted in a decline in mural activity. Although sumptuous fantasies were still painted in places throughout Europe and in churches in Latin countries, it was not until the late nineteenth

century that popular interest in murals returned.

The most astonishing development in mural art occurred in Mexico in 1920, when artist supporters of the revolution (1910-20) began a movement which in ideology, scale and quality has influenced generations of artists worldwide. The revolution aimed to erase European exploitation in Mexico and inaugurate an egalitarian society with widespread reforms. Murals, painted in magnificent government buildings and churches, developed the aims of the revolution, referred to the richness and diversity of Mexican history and explored the paradoxes and opportunities of the post-colonial situation highlighting differences of race, culture and income. The murals at first reflected the beneficial advances in education, industry, agriculture, science, technology and medicine, and later upheld the promises for re-

1

Stanley Spencer, The Resurrection of the Soldiers, Sandham Memorial Chapel, Burghclere, 1927-32.

form that the revolution had long since neglected. Their styles repudiated the conservative nineteenth century European tradition and used forms and constructions suggested by popular metalcut illustrations in newspapers, pre-Columbian art, the Spanish influence, modern European developments and the artists and thinkers of the Russian revolution.

The murals were figurative, full of colour and movement, often rich in detail and intentionally used architectural space. Perhaps most importantly, they addressed themselves to the widest possible public audience.

In the first half of this century British murals influenced similarly by Socialist ideas, showed a new interest and concern for ordinary people. Stanley Spencer painted a series of murals for Burghclere Chapel about soldiers' lives in Gallipoli in the First World War, and for the War Museum, scenes of Clydeside shipbuilders in WWII. During the 1930's artists of the Artists' International Association painted murals for trade unions and factories, returning art to the wider audience it had had before the Renaissance. This time however, instead of asserting the dominion of church and state, it was being used to assert the value of the lives of working people.

Murals continued to be painted in the post-war period. Some, like those of new schools in Hertfordshire, were commissioned by public bodies and funded through their discretionary sixpence in the pound levy for new civic buildings. Mural departments flourished in art schools like Hornsey and the Royal College in London and a society for mural painters was active. But without a sustaining philosophy or public interest both had disappeared by the late 1950's.

In the United States the Public Works Authority funded hundreds of murals during the 1930's Depression. When unemployment ceased to be a problem during the war, the Public Works programme came to a stop. Mural programmes were considered valuable by government not in contributing to the nations's culture but as token gestures towards employment problems.

Street Art

The resurgence of mural painting which began in 1967 in Britain and the USA started therefore without the support of a strong recent tradition. Moreover the new murals were being painted on outside walls in countries in which there were no such precedents. Two connected factors generated this movement. The first was that the late sixties saw the culmination of radical activity in the West, for racial equality, women's equality, and an attack on oppressive aspects of government, together with a liberating tide of alternative culture. The second was that for many artists, murals offered the opportunity to break away from the restrictions of gallery art, to take art to the streets and to a wider audience than the socio-economic group that patronises galleries. The initiative for this movement primarily came from artists, many of whom had a fine art training, but who saw the development of art through a collaboration with a neglected and erstwhile 'audience' of the arts, i.e. with 'ordinary people'. The movement also coincided with and complemented the development of community action, as architects and town planners became interested in community involvement in the initiation and implementation of planning architectural schemes or the more straightforward redevelopment and refurbishment of existing property and sites.

Housing Action areas were set up in urban areas and self-determination and self-help by community and local groups were encouraged by young professionals, eager to respond to demands made by helpful, determined and ambitious working class people. At the time painting on a wall still made people think of graffiti, and it was frowned on by officialdom. For the painters, (artists and people alike) it was a liberating experience, proclaiming their aversion to a rigid and represssive society and reclaiming walls and the environment for themselves and their fellow citizens. For the artists it was the opportunity to prove that they were artisans with a definite place in society.

A vivid accessible style, a strong underlying form, strong colours, and didactic content were typical of murals of this period. What the mural painters discovered was that art on the street demanded different skills and styles both from studio work and from the interior murals of previous generations. The design had to be adapted to the shape of the wall and the surrounding buildings, it had to be more highly charged with colour and the composition had to be both more careful and more forceful and, it had to 'read' well at distances as well as close to.

While the mural images were having to be consciously fashioned to physcially fit the built envrionment, their social role was beginning to change. Local people were becoming involved in the process of the work, participating in the whole scheme from its funding to the celebration of its completion. Indeed for many artists the involvement of local people throughout was crucial to the success of the whole project. Thus many murals depict subjects of local interest or aspiration, and contain portraits of local people, some of whom may have taken part in the design and painting processes, or in the activity the mural was depicting.

Developing this dialogue, and conscious of the potential didactic influence of their work, some muralists used murals to make political and social statements. They and others saw their work affecting the environment, using murals to trigger improvements to the locality, even proposing a package which would provide landscaping, play structures, or gardens.

At the beginning of this recent mural movement some muralists chose to work with children (the most notable being the Islington Schools' Education Project) believing them to be more receptive and less constrained by convention, and thus the artists felt they were likely to have a greater social effect. Through the process of making durable, usable images with children, often in collaboration with teachers in other disciplines, muralists have been able to make schools and youth centres more attractive and contribute to the improvement of learning skills generally.

Other muralists, such as Peter Senior with the Manchester Hopsital Project and Beth Shadur at Barlinnie Special Unit elected to work in hospitals or prisons with considerable success.

The advent of Manpower Services Commission (MSC) sponsorship of arts projects, the development of the use of mural programmes by organisations like SHAPE and the interest of certain Regional Arts Association officers gave rise to an increase in mural schemes in schools, hospitals and inner city estates and community centres in the early 1980's.

The Future

In 1978 ninety muralists attended the first National Murals Conference, possibly half the number then working in Britain. Since then the number of artists producing murals has increased enormously, working in a variety of ways ranging from community murals, through work in schools to private commissions in homes, work places and public settings.

The initiative of the community based mural scheme encouraged a resurgence of public art murals and mosaics sponsored by private patrons and corporations. Concern for the quality of the Environment has encouraged the 'Percent for Art' movement, whereby a percent of expenditure on all public building is spent on art work. It has become agreed policy for a growing number of civic authorities for their own capital building projects, and who use their planning powers to encourage and persuade the private sector to do likewise.

As the quality of murals has improved so planners have become persuaded of the contribution they make to the urban landscape, people generally speak of murals more knowledgeably and enthusiastically than before and this has led to an increase in the number of murals for public buildings year on year.

Interest in improving and maintaining the whole environment has generated concern about the life expectancy of murals. At one time it was thought that murals were transitory, because they were addressed to a particular time, and a life of five or ten years was considered sufficient. Now, because people expect murals to last longer, artists are exploring more permanent materials.

More art colleges have recently established courses or options in Public Art. Those currently on offer are: Bradford and Ilkeley, Canterbury, Chelsea, Dartington (Devon), Duncan and Jordanstone (Dundee), Glasgow, Kingston, Sunderland, Wimbledon and Winchester.

The 'Art and Architecture Group' has for several years been promoting the idea of artists and craftspeople working with architects on architectural projects. The movement continues to grow and the debate about the issue increases in intensity. Art and Architecture have a register of members from the arts, crafts and architecture, holds frequent meetings and produces a newsletter for its members. Their address is: Art and

Graham Crowley, mural at Chandler's Ford Library, Hampshire, 1983.

Architecture Ltd. Dunsdale, Forest Row, East Sussex RH18 5BD. Tel: 034282 2748.

Supermarket chains have begun to see the commercial rewards of commissioning murals, and developers continue to commission groups to paint murals for the perimeter boards of their city sites. Many advertisements for competitions, commissions and placements for artists to create public murals appear each month.

Whilst there has therefore been an increase in public art murals in recent years by contrast community murals have not prospered so well. Grant aid has declined partly because of pressure on local authorities to reduce expenditure on leisure pursuits in order to maintain essential services, partly because market-oriented policies of Regional Arts Associations deny the support they used to give working class initiatives, and because they want to take back the control of how and what is produced under their support, and partly because there is an increased interest in public art as opposed to community art.

Social concern was central to the complex philosophy of community arts in the last decade, and was the key to its success. The challenge in the nineties is for those artists involved in public art to develop as determined and persuasive an ideology. Why 'art in public places? Is it due to a concurrent move in architecture and planning to produce buildings and spaces that pay greater attention to the needs of people?; is it that the sense of involving people in the development of their environments has permeated the general thinking about where art can be most effective?; or is it pure opportunism in developing new markets to replace state sponsorship that is continuously being eroded?

Wallscapes working on their East Herts Youth Services Bus, 1990.

The public arts movement needs a strong ideology, one which enables artists to choose whether they engage in the public arena or not, which ensures that the products are vibrant and visually enhance our public places, one which extends the vocabulary and range of art, and also relates to people's needs and aspirations.

Ray Walker at work on his Chicksand St. mural.

Brain Barnes, 'The Good, the Bad and the Ugly, Battersea Bridge Approach, London, 1978. Photo: Abdul Chowdry.

3

Sponsors

In many cases murals cannot be paid for by your clients and you have to work with them or by yourself to find sponsors. Research the whole range of sources, often the project will not rely on the support of one, but several sponsors.

Sponsors have criteria for the allocation of grants, so ask each one you approach what are *their* criteria. If you have an outline of your project you can describe it to them and find out if it is the sort they might assist. Ask when the best time is to apply for a grant, whether there are specific forms to complete, and whether they are likely to sponsor an entire mural project or only make a contribution. When contacting a prospective sponsor a telephone call may be sufficient, but sometimes a visit is necessary. If you have already produced a mural, invite them to see it.

In most cases decisions about allocating grants are made months in advance, so make sure that your application is made sufficiently early to meet your prospective funder's deadline.

The format of the application to a grant agency will vary according to the information they want . Usually they will expect to see:

1. your curriculum vitae (cv) and photographs of previous work.

2. where an application comes from a group, local or professional, they will require information on past activities and a description of the project, possibly with drawings.

3. a budget: on which their contribution is shown as an item of income, and which identifies other sponsors, if any, to whom you are applying.

4. if you are applying as a group they may ask for a copy of your constitution.

The way the photographs, drawings, and written material is presented is important (see Presentation).

Some sponsorship may be 'in kind' e.g. paint, storage for materials and equipment, scaffolding, offers of help from volunteers, which can be set against the total expense in your budget. It is as well to know the financial value of such sponsorship as this will give funders a picture of the real cost of the project. It is also useful knowledge for funding future projects, because if such 'hidden costs' are not revealed, potential sponsors will assume that labour, goods and services etc., are being donated and may cut down on provisions.

Central Government

Central Government funds fluctuate according to government policy. In the past mural projects have been assisted through social and environmental partnership schemes between central and local government. At present loacal authorities (LA's) in certain urban areas may apply for the funding of a package of improvements towards employment, environment and social needs, through The Inner Area Programme. Within this umbrella it is possible for murals to play a part.

Employment training schemes have also been sources of funding for murals in the past, but this has declined of late. Money for training is available from European Community funds but this is extremely difficult to negotiate at present and does not seem a viable option. Officers of your local authority should be able to tell you of funding opportunities as they come up.

Local Authority

It is sensible to find out about your local authority, meet the council members of your ward and others who may support your project who serve on different committees or from the particular wards in which you are intending to work. Where necessary, meet the officers who advise committees and carry out their decisions.

Normally an application for a grant towards a mural will go to one of a number of committees of which the most likely are: the Arts and Recreation Committee and Community Committee, whose interest may be the development of arts activity and community involvement in that activity; the Housing Committee and the Planning Committee, whose interest may be in the provision of environmental features, the amelioration of faceless estates and the elimination of grafitti; the Social Services Committee, whose interest may be the provision of more pleasant surroundings for, or appearance of, social facilities, playgrounds, houses, etc., and the opportunity to involve particular groups in working on the project; and the Education Committee, whose interest will be the contribution murals can make to schools and colleges, both in appearance and in encouraging collective activity.

If an application is recommended for grant aid by one of these committees it usually has to go through another one or two committees for ratification.

Public Art Funds

The Arts Council of Great Britain (ACGB) no longer gives project funds for public arts since this has been taken over by the Regional Arts Associations, though it continues to promote public art and the 'Percent for Art' philosophy. It has however a fund - 'Exhibitions and Events'- for projects that are inter-regional. Thus if, for example, you are creating a portable mural to go around the country you could apply. For information on funding, see: 'Visual Arts Grants' from The Arts Council of Great Britain, 14 Great Peter Street, SW1P 3NQ. Tel: 071 333 0100.

Regional Arts Associations (RAAs), now becoming Regional Arts Boards, are funded almost entirely from ACGB, with only a small part from local authorities and other sources. Each regional authority will have a policy on the funding of murals, which may come under 'fine arts', 'public arts' or 'community arts', depending upon differing attitudes towards the purpose of murals. For information enquire from the Regional Arts Association for your area.

The Local Arts Council. Often a borough or town will have its own Arts Council which disburses funds to assist arts activities in its area, and is usually funded by the borough. For information enquire from the Secretary of the Arts Council or from your local authority.

The Royal Society of Arts (RSA), supported by The Department of Environment runs a scheme 'Art for Architecture', through which architects, developers and local authorities who are having a building designed or with a develpment under way, can apply to the RSA for a grant to employ artists or craftspeople. The intention of the scheme is to encourage the use of artists right at the start of the design process, to include the artist as part of the design team, ensuring that the final artwork is integral to the building and not an afterthought. Details from The Royal Society of Arts, 8 John Adam Street, London WC2N 6EZ. Tel: 071 930 5115.

Trusts and Foundations.

There are a number of trusts and foundations which may fund mural projects. We list the ones below because they have consistently helped, but there are other trusts and foundations which may well be supportive. The Directory of Social Change

give advice about these. See: 'Arts Funding Guide', The Directory of Social Change, 169 Queens Crescent, Kentish Town, London NW5 4DS. Tel: 071 284 4364, also:

The Handbook of Grants' by Graeme Farnell, distributed by AN Publications, PO Box 23, Sunderland SR4 8BX.Tel.: 091 5673 589.

The Gulbenkian Foundation supports the Arts . Their policy towards mural projects changes from time to time, and currently they will probably look favourably only on schemes which are part of environmental improvement. Applications and advice to applicants from: The Director, The Gulbenkian Foundation, 98 Portland Place, London W1N 4ET. Tel: 071 636 5313.

The Mural Trusts. These are two mural trusts administered by a committee at the Royal Academy. The conditions under which grants may be given are rather specific, so it is best to note them carefully. The names of the trusts are: The Vincent Harris Trust and The Edwin Austen Abbey Trust. For information enquire from: The Secretary of the Mural Trusts Committee, The Royal Academy of Arts, Burlington House, Piccadilly, London W1V ODS. Tel: 071 439 7438.

Public Art Development Trusts

There are a number of trusts in the UK whose function is to encourage the siting of works of art in public places by initiating and organising commissions from both public and private sectors. Each has a register of artists and craftsworkers and maintains a slide library of their work. Architects, developers, local authorities, commercial enterprises and others who want to commission a public work can select an artist and organise the project through the trust.They also take a role in publicising and increasing the numbers of public works and pressing for wider implementation of 'Percent for Art'. It is worthwhile registering with them. They are:

Public Art Development Trust, 1a Cobham Mews, Agar Grove, London NW1 9SB. Tel:071 284 4983.

Public Art Commissions Agency, Studio 6, Victoria Works, Victoria Street, Birmingham B1 3PE. Tel: 021 212 4454.

Art in Partnership Scotland Ltd., 233 Cowgate, Edinburgh EH1 1NQ. Tel: 031 225 4463.

City Gallery Arts Trust, The Great Barn, Parklands, Great Linford, Milton Keynes MK14 5DZ. Tel: 1908 606 791.

Sculpture North, St. Andrews, Church Street, Hebburn, Tyne and Wear NE31 1DR. Tel: 091428 0005.

Welsh Sculpture Trust, Top Floor, 2 John St., Cardiff CF1 5AE. Tel: 0222489543.

These organisations work closely with local boroughs, RAAs and private commissioners. There are other similar agencies which your RAA will be able to put you in touch with, most of whom will be part of Public Art Forum, the national association for organisers of public art programmes.

Industry and Commerce

Approach national and local industry and commerce, who may fund the project financially or 'in kind'. Paint manufacturers can be approached for all the paint and preparation materials needed for the mural, or for rejected or damaged cans. Scaffolding firms may loan or offer to put up scaffolding for the project, free of charge. Local hire firms may be prepared to loan trestles and ladders and local authorities may give or loan materials or equipment.

Whilst industries involved in the envi-

ronment might be expected to be more interested in assisting the project, local businesses large or small without such connections may also contribute financially. When approaching a firm for assistance stress that their company's name will be identified on a plaque or inscription on the wall thanking them for their contribution. They may also be interested in using photos of the finished wall for advertising purposes or in trade magazines.

Dulux run an annual competition and provide paint from their current season's stock. Information can be obtained from Dulux Community Projects Office, Welbeck Ltd., 43 King Street WC2E 8RJ. Phone 071 836 6677.

Crown Paints and J.W. Bollom Ltd. have also offered paint for murals, and it seems reasonable to assume that they are typical of many manufacturers.

Local Community Funds

Money can be raised by local organisations like youth clubs, churches, arts centres, pubs and theatres, through running jumble sales, benefit performances, and discos. 'In kind' support from the community includes volunteer labour, loan of tools and equipment, the offer of storage space, office, meeting or design space, help with transport.

Certain local authority or central government funds are available only to community-based or voluntary organisations. Do not neglect this source of funding as it is a very direct way of a community sponsoring its own mural.

Education

Working with children, young people or in further and adult education makes it possible to apply for funds from educational bodies. Projects involving children at every level of schooling and in further education would qualify for consideration for funding from the local or regional educational directorate. Projects involving youth clubs whose activities are in part supported by the education authority, should consider applying for a grant from the authority.

Mural projects in colleges might be funded similarly but since they are often more financially independent than schools it is possible that their funding sources would be different.

It is likely that mural projects will draw support from a variety of sources, even from a maintenance budget for example.

An example of long-term support gained by aggregating funds from several sources is The Islington Schools' Environment Project which was initally funded partly from teachers' salaries, partly from an Urban Aid grant where the partners were the De-

partment of the Environment and the Regional Education Authority.

Present funding for the arts is becoming scarcer and more difficult to achieve, many of the sources outlined above will be affected by the reductions in public expenditure.

Funding of the arts is an integral part of the provision of services, leading to a higher quality of life, and is as important as the funding of education and basic services. It is therefore, now more than ever before, a political issue and government both national and local need to be lobbied for their continued support.

It is also important to be on the lookout for new funding sources coming on stream as old ones dry up, and here the local authority and Regional Arts Association officers should be of help.

Brian Barnes, Riders of The Apocalypse,1983, Deptford, London

Jane Gifford, Sergio Navarro, Nick Cuttermole, Rosie Scaife-d'Ingerthorpe, Changing The Picture 1985, Greenwich, London. Photo Chris Hudson.

Greenwich Mural Workshop, Mosaic Benches, 1981, London

Dave Binnington, Paul Butler, Des Rochfort, Ray Walker, The Battle of Cable Street, 1978-83, London.

Commissions

With increased interest in Public Art has come a greater number of commissions and competitions, which range across most art media. The only criteria for entry are your enthusiasm and ability to prove your worth. Commissions come in three ways: through competitions, through publicity and through an agency. Invariably you will be in direct competition with other artists and will be judged not only on the quality of your finished products but also on your ability to sell yourself.

Clients

There are five types of client, who are:
1. Local authorities, see: 'Sponsors'.
2. Health Authorities, for work in hospitals and clinics. Two organisations giving advice to artists concerned in health care are: Arts for Health, Manchester Poly, All Saints, Manchester M15 6BY. Tel: 061 236 8916, and: The British Health Care Arts Centre, Room 5/001, Duncan of Jordanstone College of Art, Perth Rd, Dundee, DD1 4HT. Tel: 0382 23261.
3. Service industries, which include shopping centres, supermarkets, filling stations, retail stores.
4. The building professions, including architectural and civil engineering firms, and developers. Besides new buildings, external and internal, an amount of work has been available recently designing and painting perimeter hoardings on development sites.
5. Public Art agencies. See: 'Sponsors'.

Publicity

Decide how you are going to attract business. You can advertise, through 'Yellow Pages', adverts in newspapers or trade magazines, through posting your brochure or leaflets and through sending letters and telephoning. Target your client group and in your advertising identify how you can help them. See the proposal from their point of view, e.g. it will be less important to supermarket managers to be told that you draw like Michael Angelo than it is to know that your product is likely to sell more beans! Your value will vary from client to client, but will certainly include some of the following benefits: Improving the environment; Opportunity for creative expression; Development of ideas; Encouraging trade; Cultural and educational aspects of art; Value of beautiful and interesting civic landmarks; Social and individual need for a sense of place and history; Bringing people together through discussion and participation in the work; Increased tourism; Social harmony; Combating grafitti.

Trading Status

Your business may need a structure. Will you be a self-employed individual or work with a team; will you be an employer or a member of a partnership, a limited company or a co-op? Your trading status will influence how you operate and will determine your tax situation. Both local and central government fund business development agencies to advise on these decisions. 'Making Ways' edited by David Butler and available from AN Publications, PO Box 23, Sunderland SR4 6DG, has useful chapters on 'Business' and 'Promotion'

Presentation

When applying to sponsors for financial assistance, when seeking a commission from a client or when entering a competition, the content and the manner of your presentation is vitally important. You have to explain your intentions engagingly and clearly, remember some people have a fairly naive grasp of visual ideas. You have to convince them you are not only skilful, but competent. Artists are at an initial disadvantage because they have a reputation for being dreamers, unused to the realities of commercial work, and incapable of dealing with administration and administrators. You have to counter this attitude with a thorough presentation of what you have done and will do.

Consider what your clients are likely to ask for, and how your material will gain their attention, interest, and confidence. Different clients will need to be dealt with in different ways, but in general your presentation's content should cover the following:

Manner.

1. Written information must be typed well and should be clearly set out with lettraset headings to each section. Better still, typeset the information using desk-top publishing. Make sure you retain well produced photocopies.
2. Photographs should be well mounted on card, or shown in display folders of clear plastic envelopes, available in sizes from A4 to A1, together with typed titles and notes.
3. Display drawings similarly. Drawings should be in scale to the finished wall.
4. Models should be competently put together so they don't look messy or fall apart. They should be titled .
5. Slides should be sent in clearly labelled sleeves. Thoroughly rehearse a slide show before presenting it.

Content

1. Curriculum vitae. Who you or your group are, and your experience (a) as artists and (b) in related activities, e.g. administrating or assisting on projects in the Arts etc. Do not be modest, do be truthful. It is the job of a cv to convince clients of your skill, professionalism and reliability.
2. The Wall. Its size and shape. How it relates to the local environment or the building it is in. The need the mural will satisfy culturally, aesthetically, environmentally and socially.
3. Ownership and Permission. Ownership of the wall. Permissions, potential for leasing. The response of local people. Ownership of the completed mural.
4. The Process. Description of the process from consultation to completion. The time it will take. Equipment, and materials and their longevity. The theme and who decides it. The design, who decides it and who must give the go ahead.
5. Costs. The Budget.

Documentation

Reference back to previous projects is always necessary, both to inform future projects and in order to show examples of previous work when applying for future work, so keep written and photographic records of your process and product. Many muralists keep diaries of events, logging them daily or weekly. It is vital to have good documentation to support applications for grants or commissions. Many public art commissions now require applicants to first send cv's and examples of past work before even requesting design ideas for the commission on hand. It is advisable to take both black and white photographs as well as colour slides. Black and white photographs are the most useful for use in newspapers or magazines.

We have found it cheaper when taking slides of finished work or work in progress to take at least four shots of the same photograph, rather than getting copies made at a later date.

Documentation also enables you to pass on information to others attempting similar projects. The sharing of ideas and techniques between mural artists has been a particular feature of the mural movement. The maintenance of a slide archive allows muralists to teach skills and explain methodology, and also to earn by giving lectures.

Keep press cuttings relating to projects. A press story can influence the way a community looks upon a project. A favourable report can be useful in promoting future projects. Journalists frequently get interview stories wrong however, so when you have a mural 'opening' etc. invite the local newspapers, but also supply a type-written press statement giving the basic facts of the project and a black and white photograph (not a photocopy), in this way you stand a better chance of influencing if not controlling what is published.

Finance

The Budget

Costs of murals vary considerably, depending upon the size of the wall, how long it takes to design and complete the mural, how much fees or wages cost, and the expense of materials and equipment. A large mural, on a specially prepared wall, using imported paint and employing three muralists for a year, costs many thousands of pounds. But a gable end on a youth club for which the paint and scaffolding have been donated, for which fees are paid for by the artists being employed as teachers, and which is painted during a month in the summer with the help of volunteers, appears to cost much less, perhaps only a few hundreds.

Both of these projects would have at some early stage set out a budget stating probable expenditure and ascertaining income from earnings, grants, donations, and donations 'in kind' to match that expenditure. These budget statements are primarily of use to the people setting up the project, to estimate necessary fees, materials and equipment and how much it would all cost. It would subsequently enable them to ask for specified sums, materials, or services from outside agencies. The costs of 'in kind' materials and services can be valued and set down as expenditure or donated income where appropriate so that the real costs of the project are revealed.

Nothing is gained by under-estimating costs. An unrealistically costed project could finish up only half done. It is better to over-estimate, allowing for unforeseen problems, delays because of bad weather, difficulties in achieving the work rate you had expected, extra charges for materials etc.

Budget Checklist

The following is a list of possible items to be included in the estimate. Not all of them would necessarily apply in a single budget.

Income

1. **Donations**:
1.1 Wages and Fees donated (this could be broken down into full-time, part-time, specialist, etc.)
1.2 Materials donated
1.3 Equipment donated
1.4 Space donated (store, office etc.)
1.5 Transport/Printing/Administration/Clothing etc. donated
1.6 Other donations
2. **Earned income**:
2.1 Payments for work commissioned
2.2 Sales of drawings, posters, etc.
3. **Grant income**:
3.1 Government (Inner Area Prog. etc)
3.2 Arts Council of Great Britain
3.3 Regional Arts Association/Board
3.4 Metropolitan or Local Authority
3.5 Local Arts Association
3.6 Trusts
3.7 Industry
3.8 Other Income

Total £ (equals expenditure)

Expenditure

1. **Wages or Fees**:
(a) for design (b) for execution
1.1 X (number) workers at £Y (rate) per hour or week (break this into separate sections if workers, e.g. part-timers, are paid at a different rate)
1.2 National Insurance (not applicable if workers are self-employed and pay their own N.I.)
1.3 Consultation fees and specialist worker fees
1.4 Payments to contractors
2. **Materials**:
2.1 Design materials (paper, colours, etc.)
2.2 Drawing materials(pencils, chalks, etc.)
2.3 Brushes
2.4 Wall repairing materials
2.5 Paint- sealers and primers
2.6 Paint- colours
2.7 Varnish
2.8 Other
3. **Equipment**:
3.1 Hire of scaffolding
3.2 Hire/purchase of scaffolding tower
3.3 Hire/purchase of ladders, trestles, etc.
3.4 Hire/purchase of lighting equipment
3.5 Repointing/rendering tools
3.6 Hire/purchase of spray equipment
3.7 Chalk marker, Plumb bob
3.8 Buckets, plastic containers etc.
3.9 Hire/purchase sanding equipment
3.10 Other
4. **Protective Clothing**: (boiler suits, headgear, gloves, etc.).
5. **Transport**:
5.1 Costs of transporting people
5.2 Costs of transporting materials and equipment
6. **Insurance**: (Third party and Employers' Liability)
7. **Printing**: (Leaflets, photocopies, dyelines)
8. **Documentation**: (Photographic record of the project)
9. **Administration**:
9.1 Telephone, Post, etc.
9.2 Rent, heat, light, maintenance (of office, store, etc.)
9.3 Bank charges, legal fees (auditor, fee to draw up contract, etc.)
9.4 Publicity
10. **Lease on Wall**: (annual rent at £ per annum)
11. **Other:**
12. **Contingency**:

Total £ (equals income)

Payment

The letter informing you that your grant application has been successful usually encloses an acceptance form to be completed and returned, and a statement about how the money is to be paid. The acceptance form may include conditions of grant aid which will affect payment of the grant itself. Take note of and comply with any such conditions as this should ensure continued payment of the grant and avoid delays. Seek to revise any conditions that appear to be too onerous or unnecessary.

Sometimes the money comes as one sum, more usually in two or more instalments during the project. Sometimes the final instalment is not paid until the project is completed. The sponsor having made the award may have to be pressed so that the finance department gets the message to make the transaction. In some instances a final payment may only be paid on the production of a final budget or audited accounts. You need to check this carefully.

The grant may only be towards part of the costs, or to pay for a specific area of costs - in which case you may be asked to

specify how you will be able to work with less or how and where you intend to find more. In some cases the grant will only be confirmed when the remainder of the anticipated expenditure is found from other sources. Do not under-budget. Include a contingency figure to set against unexpected outgoings.

Spending

Where the mural is a project independent of an existing organisation e.g., a muralists' collective or a community arts organisation, you will need to open a bank account and to keep a set of books. It is necessary to keep watch on the progress of the project to see that you are keeping within the spending limits you have been given in the budget. Having a bank account helps to keep a check on how much is being spent.

If for some unexpected reason the project starts to cost more than the budget and economies cannot be put right, then you will have to apply for supplementary grants or fees to cover these costs. However such a facility is rarely available these days, so it is important that your project stays within budget. Where a mural project costs less than the budget estimate, the sponsor's contract with you may explain what to do; usually having made a 'once and for all' grant, sponsors will not expect to see money returned. Some may ask you to state what you intend to do with the remainder and will usually accept that the money is to be put towards future mural projects.

Accounting

Always keep accounts of all that is spent. Get invoices for all that you purchase, or till slips when you cannot get a written bill, or write out notes explaining expenditure items where you have neither of these.

Enter all items into an account book under appropriate headings (see Budget Checklist). Accounts are necessary for control of the budget to show the sponsor how their cash was spent.

Sponsors of large projects will not pay out the entire grant at one go, but will pay it in two or more instalments (so that their risk against the project failing is reduced), and they may expect to see a statement of how the money of the first instalment has been spent, before giving the second, etc. In some cases the sponsor may give a grant at the start of and during the work but withhold the final instalment until the work is complete, as a guarantee that the mural is completed. This may mean the project will have to depend on a bank overdraft for a while.

If your project is a large one, (for example, set up as a government training scheme with a lot of workers), you will be expected to submit audited accounts to your funders. Your local authority may be able to audit for you if they have an input into the project, but whatever audit is carried out you will be expected to keep the books. Remember to include the costs of an audit in your estimated budget.

If other artists are employed on a self-employed basis you need to keep a record of their name, address and Schedule D number. If they don't have one they need to fill out a P46 form, obtainable from their local tax office. This protects you from the possibility of having to pay their tax contributions should they default.

THE WALL

Over a period of years a mural can become a well-known landmark, but often the process of design and painting has been equally significant and dramatic. Here we describe the permissions, discussions, design developments and techniques of transferring the design to the wall, which make up the whole process.

Selecting a Wall

If you have been invited to do the project, the wall may have been selected already, or as with a commission there may be no choice. If there is a choice the following are some points to bear in mind.

Location: Choose your wall so that the greatest number of people will see it; choose one that can be seen from a distance as well as close to. Walls at right angles to the street are particularly easy to see as are walls on street corners, and those set back from the street across an open space. Avoid a wall that is blocked by obstacles, e.g. another close building or trees. With internal walls, select ones which are visually accessible

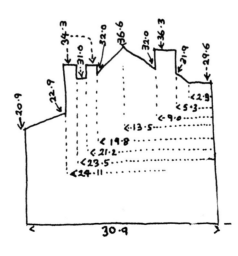

and uncluttered, and which allow the viewer to see them from a distance. A wall with restricted viewing access in a corridor will present particular design problems.

Condition: If possible try to find a wall that is new or recently repaired. Otherwise check for: crumbling, flaking or uneven bricks; mortar that is crumbling, loose, receding or sticking out from the brick; structural weakness, e.g. where the wall bows or where there are large cracks; moisture and drainage problems. Where these exist they must be repaired.

Size and Choice: Be sure you can handle the wall you select. A small wall will diminish paint costs, time, scale problems, etc. and with a low wall you can reduce problems of scaffolding and insurance.

Measuring the Wall: It is essential to have an exactly scaled drawing of the wall on which to work out designs, so it is necessary to measure it exactly. Make a sketch, fairly large so that you don't get confused by measurements later; put in doors, chimney breasts, pillars, places where the wall changes direction etc. If the wall is easily accessible then measuring it is a simple matter of using a spooled tape and reading off dimensions. If parts of the wall cannot be reached then use the 'brick-counting' method: each brick & mortar line being 3 inches high and each half-brick 4 and a half inches long; count them and multiply by three or four and a half to get the vertical or horizontal dimensions. This method is an accurate way to place elements such as doors and windows on the sketch design.

Permissions

When planning a mural there are certain permissions that you will require. In some cases such as commissions, these permissions will be arranged by the commissioning body, but it is advisable to check that all possible permissions have been obtained.

From the owner of the wall

In many instances the owner of the wall will reside in the building concerned. Obtaining permission in this case is straightforward. Where the wall is part of a school, hospital, library or other institution, the ownership will be in the hands of a public authority and it is necessary to discover just who owns the wall. You can be helped by the head-teacher or director of the building, or in difficult cases by the Planning Department of the local authority. Then permission can be obtained.

In all cases try to get an agreement that the wall will be protected from change by the owner, or a future change of owner, for a certain period. One way to do this is to take out a lease on the wall for an agreed number of years. You may have to agree to maintain the wall in good condition for the agreed lease period (see sample lease).

From the Owner of the land on which the scaffolding will stand

If the land is owned by the owner of the wall, obtaining permission will again be straightforward. Where the land is publicly owned permission will be required from the local authority. If the land includes a pavement then permission must be gained from the local authority Borough Engineers. For open space the permission would be granted by the Planning Department or the Planning Committee. Do not confuse these last two. The Planning Department is run by employed council officers, the Planning Committee is comprised of elected local councillors and is the more important.

From the Planning Authority

Permission is needed where: a) the building is in a Conservation or Development Area, b) the mural advertises. This would include decorative shop signs, c) the wall is part of a listed building.

It is worth checking whether you need planning permission with your local authority Planning Department as they tend to prefer deciding on permissions related to specific cases.

The local Planning Department will tell you exactly what permissions you require and which department of the local authority you must approach. In some cases the Planning Department may demand that it gives permission for the design as well. Unless such a demand is acceptable to you and the group you are working with, question it.

Copies of the 1990 Town Planning Act are available in your local library or the local authority Planning Department.

If Permission is refused

Try to find out why. Then try to provide arguments to persuade the person or group to change their mind. If extensive persuasion is required, involve the community you are working with, local councillors and even fellow mural artists. Methods of persuasion other than direct discussion may include petitions and lobbying council committees and local councillors. It may be advisable to have a second wall in mind when planning a project, so that if permission is refused you don't have to spend a lot of time looking for an alternative site.

In the case of a community mural all the above permissions follow the obtaining of the most important consent, of the people living in the locality.

Contracts

Example contracts are shown at the back of this book. Where both parties are agreeable to signing contracts, the insurance these represent for everyone against disagreements and misunderstandings makes them invaluable, especially when the mural is a commerical commission. In some circumstances, letters exchanged between sponsors or clients and muralists represent contracts and neither party may feel further agreements are necessary. The sponsors will state that the money is given on condiiton that a mural of a certain description will be produced, and the muralists will commit themselves to carrying out the work for which the money is given.

We have heard that some local authorities welcome the sort of contracts devised by Lydiate, others may find the contracts an intrusion and hindrance to their usual operations. We recommend the use of these contracts, especially where there is possibility of misunderstanding, disagreement or default.

Artists do not normally have a contract with the community with whom they work. However the 'final design', agreed between artists and a community represents an implicit and unwritten contract, whereby it is understood the community will not want further changes, and the artist will not make changes to the design, other than perhaps in detail.

Leasing

A protection for the continued maintenance of a mural is a lease on the wall. For a number of years we have used a lease by which the mural remains in the muralists' possession for a specified number of years and they agree to maintain it. The wall's owner agrees not to alter that part of the property without permission of the leaseholder.

Sample Lease Agreement
For..............................Muralist/Mural Group
In consideration of you paying me/us a sum of £5.00 per annum payable annually, the first payment to be made on..
I/We agree to allow you to fabricate and maintain a mural on the premises situated at.............................. ....
and known as...
on the ....(direction) facing wall. Subject as hereinafter mentioned this agreement is to remain in force for..................number years certain commencing on the following day.....................................and shall be terminable herein after at any time provided twelve months notice has been given by either party.
This agreement shall be binding on my/our heirs and successors and assigns and inure for the benefit of your successors and assigns.
Signature of the owner of the wall....
....
Address..
....
Date...
Signature of Witness...................................
Address..

Magnus Irvine: Highbury Fields Mosaic, London, 1988

Themes and Consultations

The vital requirements for any mural are that it has a positive relationship with its surroundings and that it responds to the needs and wishes of those who commission it. This puts a responsibility on the muralists to get to know their location and locality, and recognise the value of consultation which will ensure that all parties will be happy with its eventual appearance.

With private commissions, or commissions through architects, artists may expect to work to a firm brief with a given theme, or one worked out in collaboration with the commissioner. The design development process may vary, but the artist should anticipate providing sketch designs from which the eventual design will spring. This process is covered in Ostler & Field's Artists Newsletter articles of October 1984 and February 1985.

A community mural demands that the artist goes further than working to a brief. Consultation is necessary to provide the themes, and the collaborative honing down and drawing together of disparate ideas into a single explicit theme that can speak for a large number of people. Critics of this process see the results as a compromise, and by inference, not comparable to the work of individuals. We believe the opposite to be true, as collaboration extends you into areas that you may never experience individually, and demands a system of working that is difficult but ultimately exhilarating. Consultation also allows objections to be discussed

The worth of consultation to a community is its recognition of the community member's right to be involved in any process that will affect their lives or environment. It is a direct statement against the patronising way in which they are treated by governments, government officers and many professionals and it can be useful in helping to increase people's awareness and pride in their achievement, and encourages their

capacity for future action. If you do not consult people in a locality or community about a mural project you can expect justifiable action from them to prevent the project going ahead, or objection through vandalism if the mural is completed.

Eliciting a Theme

In some cases the initial contact will come from an individual or group representing a community or organisation, and occasionally they so truly reflect the consensus that design development can take place just with them.

More often you also need to discover the opinions of the larger group. Calling meetings, by leafletting or putting up posters, is one way to start contacts. It is also useful to attend community meetings as a way of getting to know an area/interest group and its concerns. Showing slides of murals at meetings helps to explain and present the intention of your project, reveals any anxieties people have about it, prepares people to discuss themes and introduces different types of styles. Because public meetings on housing estates rarely draw many people you may also need to ask local residents for themes by going from door to door.

In the case of a commercial mural or commission you may be producing sketch designs to a brief already set. It is still important that you present your designs to the client directly as there may be as many different interest groups involved in agreeing the final design as with a community project and you need to experience their particular interests at first-hand.

Whoever or however you consult, the next step is to classify and prioritise the themes which are suggested, showing the strength of opinion behind each idea, and ones which broadly agree or overlap. These then form the basis of the first sketch designs.

Variety

Muralists may come to a wall knowing what the theme will be, or they may come knowing that out of a (literally) infinite number

of possibilities a theme, or a group of related themes, must be found. At this point it would seem sensible to chart possibilities before discussing which direction to take. For example:

Issues (national): disarmament, women's rights, pollution/ecology, treatment of animals, trade, employment, multinationals, resources, law enforcement, racism, militarism, religious intolerance, media violence

Issues (local): hospital closures, public transport, education, housing workers' co-operatives, resistance to factory closures, signing on campaigns, etc. pensioners' rights, consumerism, community facilities

History: history of buildings and streets, working people, transport, communications, manufacturing industry, retailing, dress, attitudes, famous events and heroes, markets, agriculture, the river and the sea, history of race and its culture.

Leisure: sport, festivals, music, art, theatre, dance, photography, film and video, literature and publishing, children's games, rehabilitation of property, machine restoration, travel, animals, gardens, the home.

Ideals: scientific advance, working together, international co-operation, equality of opportunity, cultural advance, responsible education and health care, fair deals for children and the elderly, the handicapped, exploration, self-sufficiency, development of 'community'.

Extending the Theme

The chart can get longer or broader by expanding each category or establishing different categories, and as the potential themes develop for the mural there will be connections from one section to another. As you begin to visualise the themes, so they further expand. Such a chart can be particularly useful in working with non-visual people, or those unused to being asked for their views. If you have some ideas to feed into the discussion you get stronger responses. To ask baldly "what do you want?" is to ask for nothing, and at this point the artist must be able to initiate ideas in order to encourage participation.

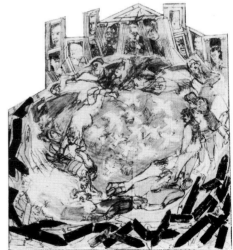

Sketch designs by Viv Howard and Steve Lobb for Creek Road Peace Mural, Greenwich, 1983.

It would be simplistic and patronising to assume that communitites bounded by a locality cannot or do not wish to be involved in wider ranging political or social issues. What is important is to recognise that issues of national or even international relevance are presented in a manner that relates to the community involved. The first discussions require empathy with, and a willingness to

discuss other people's ideas and imagination. It is useful to ask what overall atmosphere is wanted, and suggest a number of polarities to set discussion going, e.g. richness or economy, soft or hard, lively or restrained; should the mural evoke a season, and so on. When discussing themes with local people some suggestions may be simple ideas like 'exciting', 'plants', 'strong colours', which give a general sense of direction or suggest elements to be included, and which may complement more specific suggestions. In some situations people are shy of overt messages and they opt for themes suggesting several qualities.

Sketch designs

The number of first sketch designs made and presented by artists varies. Some may do three, some as many as ten; the number is dictated by the time available and the amount of discussion necessary to reach a single theme. We find it usually takes three cycles before you are down to one major theme (which may by then have other subsidiary themes within it). The next step is to develop the selected design up to a detailed final version ready to put up on the wall. Take care to develop each sketch design to the same level of detail, since those that are more specific and carefully drawn sway people's choice against those that are less well developed. As the designs are discussed you will be able to see which ones should be eliminated and which should be carried further. It is the artists' job to ensure that whatever theme is developed it is visualised in the most exciting way they can, looking constantly to pushing and developing the boundaries of mural painting and testing our established principles of art.

Occasionally themes will be suggested that the muralist would refuse, racist, or sexist themes are two obvious ones, and

many muralists may find it difficult to get enthusiastic about themes like 'Walt Disney characters' or 'a beautiful landscape', but by pushing the discussion as to why such fantasies are being suggested you may come to deeper and more exciting ideas from which to develop a mural. There are themes which are so well known or so conventional that they offer no challenge and excitement to the muralist, and both the muralist and commissioner, need to have a theme which enables them to grow.

"Above all the theme must speak to the audience, the community. If it doesn't it has no place in the public forum of a mural"
M. Rogovin / H. Highfill, 'Mural Manual' Beacon Press, Boston 1975.

The Design

This section looks at how ideas can evolve in such a way that the wall itself emphasises the theme and responds to the locality and suggests methods of simulation and ways of dealing with scale.

Size

The overpowering area of a wall can be a cause for concern. Designing on a small scale, within an outline identical to the shape of the wall, reduces the problem to a size one can handle confidently. The first sketches may be on paper only a few square inches in size. As the design develops so drawings need to grow larger in scale to take account of additional ideas and detail, and the final design might be on a scale ranging from a half inch up to two inches to a foot, depending upon the nature of the design, its complexity and detail. It is more important that the design be on a larger scale if the people who will be transferring the design to the wall are not skilled in drawing, as more detail can be included and the design is easier to transfer.

Women's Peace Mural by London Wall, 1983, designed by group collage

Shape

Walls come in a variety of shapes. Respond to the shape of the wall as a challenge. Question the impact that will be made by using the shape of the wall, and aim to use it so skilfully that it looks as if the wall was made to fit the image.

Walls are divided by columns, chimneys and recesses and interrupted by windows, doors, drainpipes etc. It is a design challenge to discover how to use them or obscure them in the design. The action of the image should take place within the given shape of the wall (with the possible exception of the lowest two feet to enable the mural to start above the damp course, or to start above where mud splashes). Murals which are designed as rectangles within the boundaries of the wall look odd, like oversized postage stamps or an advert. If you are considering only using part of the wall it is more effective to consider an irregular shape to the mural which then uses the remainder of the wall as part of the design feature. Forms or shapes in the image which do not relate to the perimeter of the wall, e.g. which are cut off by it or which go indiscriminately against the architecture, jar and disrupt the senses of the viewer.

Producing the Design

Having established a theme or a variety of themes it is important when considering the conversion of these into a design first to look at the formal divisions of the wall. This can be initially achieved through dividing the wall shape into an abstract pattern which can be translated into representational forms. The 'patterns' can be regular or irregular, uneven or repetitive. They can simulate movement, they can aim at inducing a still and quiet image or one of conflict. The possibilities are endless but the pattern should not contradict the theme. The point of formal division of the physical space is to complement the theme and also to relate the mural to the nature of the locality. An example of this might be a situation where a mural full of sharp contrasts and movements is asked for to wake up a dull area, perhaps the theme is the need for change. In another situation a symmetrical 'pattern' may be called for, which blends with the locality in organisation and colour and possibly carries a theme which deals with local history.

Pillaging the past is helpful and it is always useful to have plenty of art books, photocopies and postcards of paintings available as a source of ideas. Particularly when working with unskilled people, information such as this is a useful alternative to drawing skills so that figures and forms can be photocopied or traced, used as they are or to make collages, or modified to be included in the design. Even the overall organisation of paintings from the past may offer ideas for the organisation of the mural while the subject matter may not be so helpful. It is useful to develop an image-bank, taking photos from magazines and newpapers, photocopies from libraries, taking your own photos and making drawings of relevant subjects, e.g. a theme related to shipbuilding may require visual information on the process, general information, faces of people of different nationalities, portraits of local people, dress, plant forms, water etc. Some information may only be gathered through original research which in itself will become part of the wider experience of creating a mural.

As the design develops and becomes more settled be careful that elements of line, position, shapes, and organisation do not become dulled when enlarging it. One safeguard against this is to use photocopied enlargements. Photocopies or dyelines of the designs enable you to freely try out ideas for design improvements or colour without losing the original.

In many cases designs are produced by a team either of artists or people with varied skills. The process is more difficult than if only a single designer is involved, although equally rewarding. For example a team can probably cover more first-stage designs than an individual. The most important concern next to producing an exciting design is that everyone in the team feels they are fully involved.

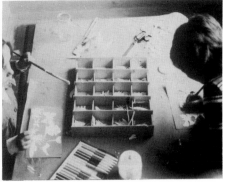
Children making designs with paper shapes.

There are many systems for coping with team work and here we mention a few. The use of photocopies of original designs allows people to work on top of other people's designs without hurting any feelings of pride or possession of the originator.

Asking different team members to

Ray Walker's drawings for Chicksand St. Mural, 1979.

produce first-stage designs initially allows everyone the opportunity to tackle the problem separately before bringing the various designs together. Dividing the wall into sections, bearing in mind the structural divisions of the wall allows individuals to develop separate sections within an overall theme.

Design Materials and Methods

The type of design materials used fundamentally affects the image produced. We would suggest that you experiment with a wide range of materials in order to encourage ideas and to carry the process of design forward from one stage to another. Crayon or gouache may be useful in quickly establishing divisions of the wall which are then worked on with pencil to achieve greater detail. These decisions need to be governed by the skill or age of the design team, how complicated the theme is, how many people are involved in the design process and the stage of the design process.

Collage is also useful in that the design can be kept very fluid with elements able to be moved and modified in reponse to discussions.

Simulation

It is often useful to make a cardboard model of the building which will carry the mural. Then when designs are made to that scale they can be tried out in situ.

Model of a Youth Centre, to show design proposals.

This not only gives you the opportunity to see the relationship between the mural and the building but also to try out colour schemes as they would relate to the surrounding locality.

Another method of achieving a realistic setting is to photograph the wall frontally, including some of its surrounds, which when enlarged can have scale designs attached to it This immediately places the design into the street context with all its own attributes of trees, buildings, people etc.

As well as being a useful tool for the design team in assessing different design options and their potential effects as realistically as possible, simulation is particularly useful for presenting designs to other people in the locality such as clients and potential funding bodies, as it facilitates the understanding of how the mural will look in reality. The more realistic the simulation the more possible it becomes for everyone concerned to identify any problems or make suggestions for changes.

Haringey Mural Workshop working on designs.

Colour

Many modern murals are colourful without using colour well in itself, colour being used mainly to clarify and intensify what is stated as a drawing. This suggests that if more time were given to explorations of colour at the design stage, then more imaginative colour schemes could be devised, giving more interesting, more specific effects and meanings. The permutations of colours offer opportunities to suggest qualities over the whole range of emotional and physical stages.

One way to explore this is to look at polarities. For example it is easy to see how sharply contrasting, strong hues will create a vivid noisy image, and how hues less strong, and close in tonal value will be more inclined to suggest harmony and softness. Experimenting with different colourways of the same original, using photocopies or prints of the original, helps to suggest and eventually, to identify the particular colour quality or meaning the mural should have. It is also useful to plunder art and design books and magazines for ideas from every period including ceramics, costumes, posters, as well as fine art, and also to collect ideas from colours in nature as well as colour photographs and reproductions.

There are four aspects to consider.

1. The character of the building will be changed by the colours used, so consider its character and how the colour should affect it.

2. Each mural relates to its specific coloured locality, one with which it will blend or stand out, and this should be examined by colour sketches or notes, and colour photos.

3. Local people have imaginative and definite views about colour, though in some cases these are only expressed when they are imaginatively canvassed. To give two examples of very generalised views: most of the people of the Garnethill district of Glasgow wanted specifically muted colours when asked by the arts team carrying out murals in 1979; in Greenwich at the same time the muralists were being told, "Bright colours definitely. No point in doing it otherwise". To some communities, as to individual clients, particular colours have symbolic importance that muralists have responded to. Sometimes these choices have a nationalistic basis but more often they are emblems of racial pride.

4. Walls get varying amounts of light according to their direction and location, and unless a mural exists somewhere without natural light, its appearance will change through the day. Dingy places created by overshadowing, interiors or subways usu-

ally demand mainly light colours for the effect of dark colours is to cut out reflectivity and make the space even darker. This does not mean using all light colours, for it is probable that in order to be seen clearly, colours need to be strong and contrasts, including tonal values, need to be wide. To give a mural good legibility at night, wide tonal value contrasts are essential.

If your mural is to be painted externally in conventional housepaints or artists' colours, or internally where the wall receives direct sunshine, you should anticipate that the paint will age after about five years. Consider therefore increasing the tonal difference and the strength of colours in your design so that the effect of fading and darkening in the mural will be less destructive to the image. The manufacturers of Polytex a popular acrylic paint in the USA, say that if less black or white is mixed with colours then there is less fading and darkening, but this assertion has not been tested with materials in Britain.

To sum up, colour should not be seen as a hazardous problem but as an opportunity in which local experience, the personality of the building, the local environment and the ambient light are important factors contributing to the design, and exploration with colouring materials using ideas both from nature and from books contributes solutions.

Onto the Wall

There are two methods of transferring the design: squaring up and projection.

Squaring Up

After priming, divide the wall into regular squares that match exactly the number of squares on the design, label each line numerically one way, alphabetically the other to coincide between design and wall. Use a metre rule and a 'Chalkomatic' plumb bob. This is a metal or plastic container available from hardware shops with coloured chalk dust and a string line inside it, which when drawn out taut and 'twanged' makes a straight line. Copy exactly what is in each square onto its related square on the wall. Normally squares would be between a foot and a yard in size. The size of the grid can vary (according to the size of the wall, and the detail of the design, etc.). The more squares you have, the more exact you can be. For areas which are detailed you can divide specific larger squares into four or more as you come to them, doing the same on your design, to make the transfer more precise.

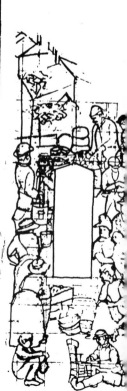

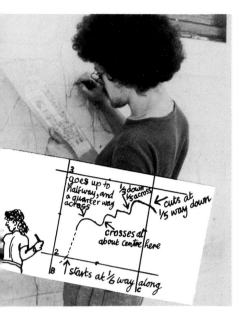

It is often useful to forget what the line actually represents as you transfer it to the wall. See it dividing its square in a particular pattern .In this way you get a true copy of the design, undistorted by your ideas of what it represents. This may seem strange until you understand the problems the sheer size of the image can bring. Make the design as clear and detailed as possible so that there is no need to be inventing and correcting later when you are painting the design. An hour spent at the design stage, deliberately working out a problem may save a day altering the image on the wall at a scale twenty times larger. This does not mean that you can't improve the design once it is on the wall.

When you have drawn up the basic design onto the wall, you can check what has been done from a distance as well as close to, and modify or add details where they are needed. But it is not wise to expect to be able to make major changes as it goes onto the wall. Take into account irregularities in the wall, first of all at the design stage. If necessary move the design to emphasise them or diminish the upset they may be causing. Can the stooping figure be shifted a foot down so that the (real) window does not cut into it? Can the drain pipe be used as a vertical constructional coloured form in the design rather than being an obstruction? Ideally problems such as this should be sorted out at the design stage but sometimes corrections are unavoidable. Some alterations may be needed to correct attitudes within the theme in response to criticism or suggestions from passers-by.Any changes at this stage should be small ones as the overall design is acting as a contract between you and your 'client', unless you have been given a free hand.

Projection

Trace the design onto clear plastic or acetate sheet using an overhead projector marker or pen designed to use with plastic; alternatively photocopy the design onto 'Copystat' acetate sheet. The design can then be projected using an overhead projector when it is sufficiently dark (it doesn't need to be at night). If your wall is small enough the design can be projected at one go, otherwise the plastic will have to be divided and the parts projected one section at a time.

To transfer a design high onto a wall the projection itself has to be from a high point, and this may require a moveable tower. Slide projectors have also been successfully used to project designs, but since this involves photographing the design onto slide and ensuring that the image on slide is sufficiently sharp, and since the projector may have to have special lenses to avoid distortion, this can be a difficult system to use.

Drawing

The sort of drawing material used fundamentally affects the final look of the mural. Clutch pencils are very precise, alterations have to be erased. Chalk and charcoal give a quicker, more rounded line. A paint line is more fluid, and likely to give the most ambiguous indication as to where colour should go. Some artists have used a fairly thick black painted outline which, even when slightly overpainted with colour, still gives a sharp outline to the separate elements of the mural.

Painting

Put paint on with love and care. We have seen murals created by people without much drawing or design skill, which have succeeded and merited a lot of attention, because they cared for it and were determined to make an excellent job of painting it. On the other hand we have seen good murals spoilt by casual daubing. The fact that murals are often large is no excuse - sloppy painting shows! Be professional, be meticulous and passionate in your painting!

Cleaning and Repairs

The materials and equipment required to carry out the painting of a mural can appear to be a deterrent, but technically a mural follows the same process of preparation, priming and painting that is used for easel paintings and for household painting and decoration. Here we describe the preparation of the wall (sometimes called the substrate), the use of conventional artists or housepaints, the tools and equipment you can expect to use and problems of maintenance.

Replacing decayed mortar lines.

To give a mural a long life it is essential to prepare the wall surface thoroughly. Your aim should be to make a firm, dry and clean surface that will encourage the primer to adhere.The more uniform the surface the stronger the paint film will be, and the more effective the painting.

Brick, Concrete, Render, Plaster

1. Remove loose and cracked paint, dirt, loose or crumbling mortar, plaster or brick, by wire-brushing or scraping. Scrub with scrubbing brushes or brooms and water.

2. Holes and cracks have to be filled, or they will appear as dark spots on the mural and allow damp to get behind the paint

Replacing decayed mortar lines

Use of Keeps coach paints on metal shutters.

with holes and deep mortar lines where the mortar has fallen away, or covered with projections where the face of the wall has decayed and crumbled. In these cases it may be quicker and better to render the entire surface than to fill or smooth it.

5. Where a wall has been damp there are usually algae, lichens or small green plants growing, frequently appearing to be no more than a green, brown or black stain. These must be removed before you can prime the wall, or they will grow again through the paint surface

First they should be scraped or wire-brushed off, then either a Fungicide or a Household Bleach (diluted 1 part bleach to 3 of water) should be brushed on, left for 24 hours and then rinsed off. If necessary repeat this until all trace has gone.

Moisture causes the deterioration of the materials of which walls are made and affects painted surfaces by washing out the pigment, by breaking up the paint film, and encouraging mould and algae to grow. It is important therefore to find the source of moisture in the wall and treat it to stop it recurring. Watch for signs showing where damp is, or has been present, such as algea growing, where mortar or brick has crumbled away, where timber has swollen and warped or where previous paint has lost contact with the surface or is discoloured.

Where the source of moisture and/or its solution are hard to find, ask for advice from an architect or a surveyor, possibly through the architecture department of your local authority. Where the solution is going to be too expensive (it may be beyond your budget) ask the owner of the wall or the local authority for assistance.

film. Large holes in brickwork, concrete and render should be filled with mortar, e.g. in brick walls where the old mortar has fallen out, it should be repointed. Large holes in plaster should be replastered and smaller holes can be filled with a paste filler such as Polyfilla or Solvite.

3. Bumps projecting from the wall should be removed by chipping or sanding

4. In some cases a wall will be pitted

Timber: Including Ply, Chipboard etc.

Timber is cellular and porous, it is also pliable and its corners and edges are easily chipped.

In contact with damp or oil-based substances it swells, distorts and under pressure will warp. So in preparing timber surfaces, see that they are protected from damp and oil, that they are well supported and that their edges are not in a position to get damaged. Where plywood is to be used outside, it must be exterior grade.

1. Where the surface has been previously painted and the paint is cracked or loose it should be removed. A previous firm but shiny paint film should be sanded to provide a key.

2. Holes and cracks should be filled with a paste filler, then sanded until smooth.

3. Where screws are driven in, heads should be countersunk and painted with an oil based primer or filled over with a paste filler.

4. Dirt and dust should be removed either by wiping with a damp cloth or by washing with a solution of cleaning agent. Grease can be removed with white spirit.

Metal

1. Corrosion in the form of scale and rust can be removed by wire-brushing and scraping or sanding. The prevention of corrosion returning is directly linked to the thoroughness of this initial cleaning.

2. Where the surface has been previously painted, sand or scrape off where it is loose, and if it is smooth to give it a key for the primers. Then clean off oil and dirt as before.

3. Clean off dirt, dust, or oil with a cleaning agent.

A top projecting wall.
If moisture is coming through the back of the wall : a) repoint if the mortar has rotted
b) check the joint between roofing and wall and repair if necessary with mortar or roofing compound.

Rain that has penetrated the wall from above when evaporating in dry weather assaults the paint from behind.
Repair the top surface of the wall or put a protective layer of mortar, tile, stone or roofing felt over it.

Rain which enters the front of wall through cracks.
Dampen the cracks and fill with mortar.

Rain or condensation which runs a particular course down the wall causing wear, discolouration and plant growth.
a) Repair the gutter or sill which should direct or channel the water.
b) Treat algae with bleach.

Rain which enters through imperfect seals between doors/windows and the wall.
Repair cracks and holes with caulking compound e.g. Evostick mastic.
N.B: Where timber is rotten with damp, cut out that area and replace.

A wall retaining soil.
Where soil cannot be removed, the solution is to put an impermeable layer between the earth and the wall.

Holes in bricks need filling.
Uneven brick surface needs rendering.

Mortar, crumbled away, needs racking out and filling.

Moisture which enters the wall from beneath. The reason for this is that either the wall lacks a damp-proof course or that the DPC no longer functions. A new DPC has to be made.

Cracked mortar needs chipping back to good and replacing.

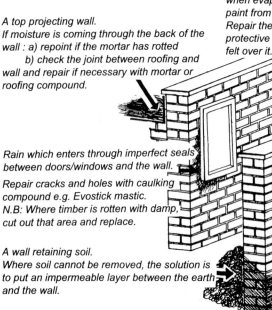

Paint Systems

A paint system can comprise from two to four separate types of paint : primer, undercoat, colour coat and varnish. The systems described here are those generally suggested by manufacturers of house paints. As far as possible, whichever system you decide upon, use paints from one manufacturer, so that you can be sure the paints are compatible. But where the best materials are too expensive do not let that deter you from using whatever is available. When it comes to deciding the particular paints for your wall we suggest you get a paint specifier from the manufacturer and/ or ask for direct advice. Some firms have consultants who give free advice on site.

An example of a design format which aims at a gentle fading of the the mural in keeping with the brick structure. ISEP's School Mural, Islington, London.

Painting on damp walls should be avoided wherever possible, but if it is unavoidable, use only acrylic or emulsion based primer, colour and varnish, because oil paints will not adhere to damp surfaces, and as they are not permeable, will not allow a wall that has become damp to dry out in dry weather without becoming badly damaged. With each application of paint always brush it on evenly, covering all the surface thoroughly. This will create a much stronger paint film and better legibility of the image.

Primers

The first paint applied to the surface is a primer, whose function is to grip the surface firmly, provide a base for further paint, and shield subsequent coats of paint from chemicals on the wall surface.

Colours

Obtain colour charts from manufacturers before you make your selection of colours. If your mural is outside check that all colours are exterior grade. Some artists colours, 'Vinyl' emulsions and 'Eggshell' oil paints are intended for interior situations only. Each of the large British paint manufacturers supply the same range of colours, selected from the British Standard 4800 range, plus a few special colours which are unique to their individual company. It is better to get strong colours in all the hues you want rather than weak colours, you can mix weak colours from strong but not vice versa.

It is likely that you will find that none of the large manufacturers stock a sufficiently wide range of strong colours - none, for example, stock a strong dark green, lemon or crimson - so you will need to go to a smaller manufacturer, if not for all your colours, at least for some of them. If you need to order the paints before the design is resolved, then get a balanced range of strong colours plus black and white, i.e. ultramarine, cobalt, cerulean or monastral blue, purple, vermilion, crimson, orange, chrome yellow, lemon yellow, viridian green, brown. If you find particular mixed colours which you would like to use from catalogues, for instance an orange yellow or a mauve, get them.

Because any mixture of colour is less strong than the colours that combine to make it, it follows that the wider the range of strong colours you have the better. It is impossible, for example, to achieve a strong dark red without using crimson, it is far better to use a manufactured purple rather than mix red and blue. The wider the range of strong colours the wider are the permutations of mixing and the better the opportunities for adventurous colour schemes.

Mixing

The staining power of hues varies. For example, red has a greater mixing power than yellow. In a mix of the two, equal quantities would produce a colour still red rather than orange and to produce a mid-orange it might require four times as much yellow as red. Similarly, a mid-grey might require six times as much white as black. Since equal quantities of paint rarely produce an equal middle, each mix has to be judged visually taking account of your experience of the staining strength of the different colours. This inequality between colours affects the total quantities of each hue you need in the mural, as you will need proportionally less of powerful stainers like black and red and more of weak stainers like yellow and white.

Within each paint system colours are intermixable. All emulsion paints are water-based and will mix together and, although there are differences in consistency, so will

all oil bound paints. It is reasonable to expect solvent-based paints to inter-mix as well, no matter who the manufacturer is. You cannot mix emulsion with oil paints, nor either with solvent-based paints The danger in mixing between manufacturers is that quality of paints vary widely. The best will be densely pigmented and have a strong binder enabling the paint to be extended with medium without reducing its adhesion to the wall, the worst will not be so well bound and will be full of fillers. Chemical structures also vary and manufacturers warn against inter-mixing. For the muralist this poses a problem, for whilst it is often necessary to get colours from different manufacturers in order to get a complete range at a reasonable cost, there may be a risk to the permanence and longevity of the completed work.

When experimenting in mixing a particular colour, mix very small quantities, to work out which basic colours to use. The fewer colours used in any mix the better, only use four colours if three will not achieve

Use of mixed media: paint, glass mosaics, trellis and planting. Freeform's 'City Garden", Hackney, London.

the right results, or three colours if two will not do, etc. If you begin a mix and it starts to go wrong, stop; start again from scratch, because probably at least one colour is destroying the mix and should not be used at all.Keep a note of colours and proportions needed to obtain the mixed colour to aid future mixing and matching

Having sorted out the basic colours required to mix a particular colour, always mix more than you are going to need. If you are mixing for one area, try to predict if you are going to be using the same mix for other areas. In this way you can be sure to have sufficient of the correct colour for all areas and will not waste time re-mixing. Keep these mixed colours in sealed cans, or jars.

Because murals are generally much larger in size than easel paintings and have irregular edges, it follows that all decisions about design have to be worked out before

Use of artists acrylics. Detail of mural by Gavin Jantjes and Tam Joseph, Brixton, London

painting. The 'painterly' process of altering the image as it proceeds does not work although improvements can be made to small scale elements of the work or details. This does not mean that the painting process is mechanical and uncreative, as inventions and decisions are continuosly being made about the shape and colour of elements which, however detailed the original design, have not been predicted.

Most failures occur in murals not at the design stage so much as where there has been a lack of care, skill or creativity at the painting stage. The root of this lies in the belief that because the wall is large, rough workmanship will be hidden. In fact, attentive, imaginative and careful painting is as important on a large wall as on a small canvas. A mural is communicating not only from a distance but close to.

Quantities

Estimating how much paint you need depends on how far the paint will spread and how many coats will be applied. Spreading capacity is always printed on the paint can (or in the manufacturer's colour chart) telling you what area the contents will cover on surfaces of average porosity. If the surface is rough and absorbent, such as rough brick, then calculate that you will need up to twice as much paint as for an average surface. Calculate the areas to be covered by each colour and areas where the colour is mixed to produce another. If you think you will need to paint areas twice, take this into account and increase amounts. Also add a percentage of the total amount needed to provide for wastage.

Varnishes

Varnishes are also oil or emulsion based, and frequently your choice is decided by the paint system used. Clear emulsion varnish or PVA,s may tend to 'cloud' in wet weather. Many varnishes do not have a long life and new coats may need to be applied every two years. On emulsion colours, which are naturally matt, and on matt oil colours,oil based varnishes give a gloss effect and enhance contrasts. The gloss effect of emulsion varnish on top of emulsion colours is much less marked.

Varnish gives the mural a protective coating, enabling the mural to be washed clean, protecting it from being marked. Its most effective use is the protection of the image from potential graffiti as this will be the layer that is removed first when cleaning off graffiti with any solvent. Careful cleaning can leave the paint colours unaffected or at the worst only slightly faded, requiring only retouching and revarnishing. The argument against the use of resin varnish externally is that it produces a layer that stops the wall from breathing, i.e. prevents water vapour passing through it. It is likely to cause the paint to crack and peel.

Anti Graffiti

We have used two anti-graffiti protective varnishes:

'Shield' made by Dimex Ltd.,116 High Street, Solihull, West Midlands B91 35D which protects wall surfaces from graffiti with two clear skins of varnish. Graffiti is taken from the surface with one of the company's cleaning solvents. The upper skin is removed but the under one remains. Subsequently a coat of the upper varnish is reapplied.

Two two-pack varnishes , EP304 and UR518, made by Fosroc Ltd, Pitfield, Kiln Farm, Milton Keynes MK11 3LX. These varnishes create an extremely hard, resistant surface from which graffiti can be removed with the company's solvent. There are many other anti-graffiti varnishes on the market, water, oil or solvent-based, which may perform equally well. Before buying any varnish ask for technical information about it, explaining the context in which you wish to use it, and ask for a sample pack to be sent for you to try out.

Paints

If you are looking for paint manufacturers then The Paintmakers Association, Alembic House, 93 Albert Embankment, London SE1 7TY, Tel: 071 582 1185, publishes a list of its members. Information about the use of particular paints, and general advice about specific problems can be obtained by phoning manufacturers and asking for the Technical Advice Department. Major paint manufacturers will supply a 'Paint

Specifier' or 'Specification Sheets' which give full information about their properties and how to deal with many different surfaces. However it is well to remember that these are commercial suppliers, that it is their business to encourage people to reuse their products after a given period of time and they have little experience of the use of their paints in unusual circumstances. Nevertheless we have found their technical departments extremely helpful.

Commercial Suppliers

Some of the major suppliers holding a full range of paints from emulsions to specialist industrial finishes, are:

AKZO Coatings 99 Station Road, Didcot, Oxfordshire.OX11 7NQ.Tel: 0235 815141. Manufacturers of Silkkens and Permaglaze.

J.W. Bollom & Co. Ud., P.O. Box 78, Croydon Road Beckenham, Kent BR3 4BL. Tel: 081 658 2299. Produce 'Bromel' and 'Keeps' Paints in a wide range of colours. Also signwriters enamels and cellulose paints.

Craig & Rose.Plc., 172 Leith Walk, Edinburgh, EH6 5EB.Tel: 031 554 1131.

Crown - Berger Decorative Products Ltd., P.O. Box 37 , Crown House, Darwen, Lancs BB3 OBG. Tel: 0254 704951.

Dulux, Decorative Sales Office, ICI Paints Division Wexham Road, Slough SL2 5DS. Tel: Slough 31151.

MacPherson Paints Ltd., Radcliffe Road, Bury, Lancs.,BL9 9NB.Tel: 061 764 6030

Artist Colours.

Artists colours are of better quality and much more expensive than household colours. Prices of colours vary considerably but all manufacturers will supply a colour chart and price list on request. We list here three manufacturers that provide good quality acrylic paint in reasonably sized containers, i.e. 946 ml. upwards, and from suppliers throughout the U.K. Both Spectrum and Daler - Rowney will give technical advice over the telephone. Of the three suppliers, Liquitex is the most expensive.

Most artists manufacturers have ceased supplying oil colours in large quanties. Consequently the largest sizes are tubes of about 250 ml., except for Spectrum who supply litre sizes in student grade oils.

Daler - Rowney Ltd., Southern Industrial Area, P.O. Box 10, Bracknell, Berks. RG12 4ST. Tel: 0344 424 621.

Liquitex UK., Ampthill Road, Bedford MK42 9RS. Tel: 0234 360201

Spectrum Paints Ltd., 259 Queens Road, South Wimbledon, London, SW19 8N Tel: 081 542 4729.

Tools and Equipment

The size and complexity of the tools and equipment you need vary considerably from mural to mural. One may need only brushes and buckets; another may need five flights of scaffolding and a spray unit as well. Where you cannot borrow tools and equipment, most small pieces will need to be bought, whilst larger pieces can be hired. Only buy equipment when you are sure you can use it often enough to make its purchase worthwhile, or if it is cheaper to buy outright than to hire and you have the space to store it for future use.

Plant and tool hire companies charge between 10% and 20% of the cost of equipment as a returnable deposit. Hire charges are made on a weekly basis, with proportionally dearer charges if you hire by the day.

Observe safety regulations in the use of your equipment.

Once you have bought or hired any equipment the responsibility for how it is operated is yours alone. Keep your working area tidy for safety as well as efficiency. Don't use equipment that is damaged, and make sure that all access equipment is strong and firmly placed. Fixed scaffolding should be erected and taken down by professional scaffolders. When using power tools it is advisable to wear goggles, earmuffs and/or masks; essentially whatever protective clothing is necessitated by the equipment or materials being being used.

Cleaning Tools

Wire brushes are used to clean loose material, dirt, old paints etc. off all types of surface; the most effective have dense wire bristles and a spade-shaped metal front with which you can scrape away loose material when brushing fails to dislodge it.

Brooms are needed to clean the wall and sweep the site, scrubbing brushes are used for all types of wall surfaces, particularly where dirt has penetrated deep down.

Orbital sanders clean walls where there is so much work to be done that brushing by hand would take too long. Sandblasting cleans walls very quickly and completely but since the equipment is large, and the process complicated and dirty, it is better to engage a sandblasting firm.

Repairing Tools

Trowels are used for replacing mortar, filling holes in brickwork, rendering plaster and wood; floats for replacing and smoothing areas of render, concrete and plaster; painter's knives are used for scraping off old paint, mixing and applying filler, and palette knives for stirring and mixing paint. Always clean any tools immediately after use.

Painting
Brushes

All brushes tend to wear out quickly on mineral surfaces and you may well have to buy a new set for each new mural. Even so, it is cheaper in the long run and gives better results to buy good quality brushes, provided you keep them in good condition.

Housepainter's brushes of 3 inch and over are used to cover large areas quickly, especially for priming and varnishing. Smaller ones, between a half inch and one and a half inches are easier to handle, get to awkward places better and are more suitable for colours. Fitches (hog-haired artists' brushes), either round or flat, a quarter inch up to one inch, are essential. Sables are used for the sharpest lines and details. They should be springy, fat and regular in shape, with a good point. Buy from size 6 upwards, looking for a modest priced range .

Paint Rollers

The large lambswool or acrylic type of roller is preferable to sponge. Rolling generally covers faster than brushing and can be used for priming any reasonably smooth surface, leaving a good texture to take the ensuing colours.

Clean brushes and rollers immediately after use with the appropriate solvent, then wash out with washing up liquid and hot water. Brushes left uncleaned or standing in white spirit or water will get a hard paint layer that is impossible to remove without damaging the bristles. If this does happen then clean them using a paint brush cleaner or paint remover.

Spray Units

Choose a unit with sufficient paint capacity and power to cover your surface fairly quickly. Often units will apply paint at an enormous rate and it is common to discover that the act of painting takes less time than the time taken in masking off areas beforehand and cleaning up afterwards. Time and labour are saved by spraying on large uncomplicated and fairly smooth areas, but on small complicated or rough surfaces it is often better to use a brush. Assume that spraying will consume 10% more paint than brushing. Use protective clothing, mask and goggles.

Access
Trestles

There are varying sizes of trestles. The one on the right of the illustration above are double rising trestles. When the legs are fully extended up to 2 metres the muralists can reach to a height of about 4 metres. Lightweight staging is recommended across the top of the trestles

Step Ladders

The best of these are about 2 metres, usually in tubular steel which can be ad-

justed to work as straight flight ladders. Ensure that these are of very sturdy construction, lighter ones are less safe and will not last. It becomes very tiring to stand in one restricted position, so ladders are not recommended for long periods of work. If you are working up a ladder take 'exercise breaks' occasionally to ease the strain.

Straight Flight Ladders

These should be sufficiently long to reach the height needed, light enough for two people to handle, and small enough to store and transport. Ladders are either a single unit, or in combinations of two or even three sections, enabling them to be used either as one to reach a good height or split so that the seperate parts can be used independently at lesser heights.

Scaffolding Towers

Towers are made of either steel or alloy, the latter being easier to handle but more expensive. Sections vary in size and weight, tower widths usually range from 4

feet to 10 feet. Heights are restricted to four times the base width, except where outrigger supports allow the tower to extend further upwards to four times the distance between the outrigger feet.

Scaffolding boards designed to fit firmly into the dimensions of the tower make up the working platforms. Assembly of towers differs according to size and weight, but one would expect a sixteen foot high tower standing on a 4 foot square base to take approximately twenty minutes of two person's time to erect, and the same time to dismantle

Fixed Scaffolding

Fixed scaffolding is hired rather than bought. Hire charges are estimated initially for the whole project, paying extra by the week for any over-run. We would recommend using a reputable scaffolding contractor who includes the costs of both erecting and dismantling in their charges. If you hire scaffolding that you erect yourself it is advisable to have the completed scaffold checked by an experienced person.

Always check the scaffolding each day before begining work to see that nothing has been moved or loosened.

The height of a lift (stage) is usually about 6 feet. If this is too low for convenient working ask for it to be increasased by 6 inches. The scaffolding should preferably touch the wall in as few places as possible. Normally the scaffolding transoms will butt right up against the wall and some ends may be inserted into the mortar for stability. In addition the scaffolding will be attached to bolts specially inserted into the wall. Where this occurs repairs, priming, painting, and varnishing will have to take place as the scaffolding is removed, using quick drying cement to fill any holes, and drying off emulsion primer and colours with a hair dryer. If oil paint is used its slowness in drying will not allow more than one coat of paint to be applied.

Main points to ensure are as follows:

1. That the scaffolding has at least a four-board wide working platform and that it is closely boarded on every lift, i.e. there are no gaps between boards.This will avoid you having to move boards from one lift to another and give free access to all parts of the mural at any time. It will be slightly more expensive.

2. That there are guard rails and toe boards.

3. That the scaffolding is securely and physically tied to the building by bracing around the edge of the wall; through windows; by being wired to 'hilti anchor' bolts set into the wall; or by buttressing from the ground .

4. That the tops of ladders are wired onto the scaffolding.

5. If the scaffolding is over a pavement and/or is on a road edge, it must be lit by bulkhead lights to protect pedestrians and to warn traffic at night, and directions and permissions for this are given by the Borough Engineer. Electricity can be connected to street lighting, provided the Council and Electricity Board agree.

Estimates

Scaffolding contractors will give free written estimates for the cost of hiring their services, and will usually hold to that cost for three months.

Insurance.

Always take out Employers' Liability (if you are employing people) or Personal Liability , both against injury to workers, and Third Party Liability , against injury to other people.

Municipal Mutual Insurance is one firm that offers this cover to mural projects. MMI Ltd, 25 Old Queen St, London SW1.Tel: 071-222 8177.

We also advise that you read government advice and regulations about health and safety at work, and get advice about any relevant government regulations about scaffolding, see:

U.K. Government Regulations: Health & Safety at Work Booklet 6.D.,and, Statutory Instrument1966 No. 94. Reference British Standard Code of Practice L. P. 97 part 2. Both available from Her Majesty's Stationery Office.

Maintenance

Interior murals last much longer than external ones, and some materials are obviously more permanent than others. There are encaustic, mosaic and fresco murals some of which are more than two thousand years old and survive in good condition. External murals properly executed in mineral paint or mosaics will last indefinitely, provided they are not vandalised; and internal murals painted in colours guaranteed for permanence, provided they are on a sound, dry substrate and are protected from direct sunlight and a damp atmosphere should last a lifetime.

Conventional housepaints or artists colours have a limited life when used externally. *How* limited is difficult to say, and it is difficult to estimate accurately how much a mural will cost to maintain. One of our murals painted in household emulsions starting fading and cracking after five years, whilst another using the same system is still in good condition after fourteen years. The first had to be erased, and the second may with careful maintenance continue for a few more years.

Assessment

It makes sense to ask the local council for assistance with maintenance, so that they understand that local communities are concerned to conserve and protect murals in their area, and to recognise that this aspect of the environment is as important as any other amenity or facility they maintain. You could recommend the expenditure of two days work plus materials each year per mural. In Belfast some 'King Billy' gable ends are fifty years old, having been carefully repainted time after time. Check with your client and/or the local community that they wish to preserve the mural in this way before you proceed. Assess the extent of the maintenance you will undertake before you start, for example by taking 'ladder high' views of the mural. This will enable you to see if it needs totally repainting, repainting in part or simply washing. It also means that you can estimate the cost of repairs.

The desire to maintain a mural is not just related to its physical condition. Whilst at the outset of a project the theme of a mural may well have been designed to be pertinent for a limited period of time, people become attached to and wish to preserve murals in their area, often wanting them maintained long after their good life has past. The quality of the paint, the physical condition of the wall, its orientation and the climate all govern the life of a mural. Its enemies are ageing, damp, rain and sunshine, pollution and graffiti.

Ageing

In external conditions, manufacturers of household paints expect them to last five years, after which the paint film will begin to break down, fade, crack or peel. Cracking doesn't necessarily require you to repair the wall immediately as we have found that the image holds together from a distance even when the paint has crazed quite extensively. But once the paint begins to peel then this must be repaired immediately to prevent further deterioration. The effect of rain and sunshine together is to erode the paint film causing fading, darkening and reduction in the strength of colours. This can also be seen as a way of allowing the mural to disappear gradually and is viable as long as the paint does not peel. Our cities are full of painted adverts from the early 1900's, gently and decoratively fading into history.

Damp

Damp in the wall causes paint to decay. If you can cure the source of damp then do so, re-priming and repainting once the wall has dried out. If you cannot, then use acrylic or emulsion paint on its own (without an oil varnish). This will enable moisture to pass through the paint film; oil bound materials prevent this. Even so the life of the mural will be relatively short. Sometimes damp in the wall is caused by moisture getting behind the paint film where the surface has not been completely covered.

Effects of damp; mural in Holborn, London:

When a decayed paint film has lost its adhesion to the wall it has to be removed by sanding or wirebrushing. The wall then has to be reprimed and repainted. Where it adheres but has changed colour, simply repaint. If the surface is very smooth or there is a top varnish coat, rub the surface down with sandpaper to give a key for repainting.

Pollution

Murals beside major roads are particularly affected, both by becoming dirty quickly and in the deterioration of the paint surface from exhaust fumes. Washing with water and detergent removes dirt and reduces the rate of decay.

Graffiti

This is not normally a problem if local people have been involved in producing a mural and if the image is detailed at ground level. But if you paint a mural that is making a forceful statement, for example attacking racism, then anticipate that its opponents will respond and that you may well have to spend time cleaning the wall. Graffiti can be removed, and there are several cleaning agents:

1. Detergent and water.
2. White spirit.
3. Acetone: available from chemists;

use either neat or diluted with white spirit. It is highly inflammable, toxic and on evaporating induces extreme cold, so take care.

4. Silk-screen general cleaner. It is inflammable and toxic.

5. Paint stripper. Also inflammable and toxic.

6. KeimFarben make a solvent, 'Dispersionsentferner', to clean graffiti from murals painted with their mineral paint. Because of the coarse texture of the render, graffiti may be difficult to remove.

7. Graffiti removers. These are provided by companies marketing anti-graffiti varnishes (see under Varnishes).

'Permanent' Systems

Artists, funders and local communities are all interested in materials that will last much longer than conventional paints. Here we describe the painting processes of Fresco and Keim, which bind with the substrate to create a surface of great permanence. We also look at other processes of mosaics and tile-making which not only produce distinctive images but pose particular problems for artists to solve and in addition release creative skills in people convinced that they cannot paint or produce artistic products.

Keim Paint

Keim, the best known mineral paint is made by Keimfarben of Augsburg and has been in use in Germany for nearly a century. Desmond Rochfort and David Binnington used it on their Westway Murals in West London in 1977 and since then other muralists have followed suit. Keim claim extraordinary longevity for their paint, a promotion brochure shows a facade seventy years old in near perfect condition. It is long-lasting, maintenance free and moreover, whilst enabling the wall to 'breathe', also protects the wall from water penetration. There are thirty-one colours in the Keim range, all except two of them guaranteed not to fade in external conditions, and though it is less brilliant and complete than an acrylic range, nevertheless striking colour effects can be achieved.

System A

The substrate should be a cement rendered surface which ideally would comprise a scratch coat covered by a top coat of nine parts washed river sand, two parts lime and one part cement, wood float or sponge finished to make it more porous. The substrate is etched twice with dilute acid, Atzflussighiet, and washed, then primed with a white primer. The paint is diluted to the consistency of milk, from its initial clayey state, and the area to be covered is dampened with a diffuser spray. Colours can be diluted further and the density of colour built up through a series of washes, however this is time consuming and requires a level of expertise that may not be present if engaging members of a local community painting their own mural. When the colours have dried they lie as powder, like pastel, in the suface. Rain does not remove them, but they can be modified either by sponging or brushing off, or by over painting. The paint is fixed by spraying with a silicate based fixative which crystallises, locking the pigment into the surface.

Keim costs about six times more than conventional emulsion or gloss paint. However if you consider that the mural is going to be valued by the community, or local authority, or client above 10 years, then the fact that Keim will not deteriorate and (graffiti apart) will require no repairs, makes it worthwhile. Secondly, if your costs of scaffolding, design and execution are going to be high, then the cost of Keim within the budget compared to conventional paint will not seem so great. Using this system a mural of 10 x 10 metres would cost approximately £2000 of which a quarter would be the cost of etch, primer and fixative. The cost of rendering is currently about £15 per square metre.

System B

The substrate can be any mineral base, such as cement rendering, concrete, stone or brick, as long as it is sound, dry and absorbent, and does not contain gypsum. The wall should be sound and prepared by cleaning, removing any previous paint, dirt, algae or oil. New rendering needs to be cleaned with a lime remover, a white primer is then painted onto the wall. In this system, the colours arrive as dry pigment, are mixed into the fixative, and once painted on become permanent and weather resistant within a few hours, so alterations to the image have to be made by overpainting. It has a slightly reduced colour range and is not so flexible as System A, but offers similar colours and permanence, and it is cheaper.

Keim, being painted on a render with a raised nap is vulnerable to graffiti attacks. Keim offer a preparation Biostrippa which enables graffiti to be removed with a hot water jet. It may also be possible to protect the surface with an anti-graffiti varnish.

Keim Mineral Paints Ltd., Muckley Cross, Morville, Bridgnorth, Shropshire, WV16 4RR. Tel: 074 631543.

GMW's Keim painted 'Wind of Peace', 1983.

Fresco

Fresco is a technique of painting, using pigments diluted in water onto a surface of fresh plaster, which is very durable in warm, dry climates. It has a reputation for decaying here in Britain, despite the fact that medieval frescoes can be seen more or less intact in many churches. Traditionally, the dry wall is first prepared with a coat of coarse lime and cow hair plaster, which is then covered with a coat of lime plaster using a finer sand. Onto this surface the design sgraffito is drawn. Then each day the artist puts on a one-eighth inch coat of plaster, sufficient to paint for that day, pounces charcoal through perforations along the lines of a tracing of the design, (to re-establish the drawing) and paints. To combat the twin enemies of damp and rapid thermal change, a recent fresco, at All Saints Middle School, Northampton, was prepared on expanded metal on steel framework bolted to the wall.

Mosaics

The range of colours in the 20mm. square glass mosaic is extensive. At the time of writing, most suppliers import their mosaics from a single company 'Vetricolor' in Italy. Whilst in Italy a range of over a hundred colours is available, the range offered in the UK is around seventy. The surfaces of the tiles are not absolutely flat and they gain luminosity from their sheen and translucency. Their uniformity hinders naturalism, even in the most 'realistic' images, e.g. Roman and Byzantine, the patterns of repeated square tiles is strong, and produces a bold and idiosyncratic image. The way the pattern is used, following the perimeter of the picture or following the form of the subject being described, is an important aspect of the process. People whose creativity is stifled when using paint often find mosaic more rewarding since they are using a material less malleable than paint and one which encourages their feeling for pattern, colour and more definite graphic decisions.

Chris Cardale working on the pavement mosaic he made with local school children in Lewisham.

Mosaic on site

The image is drawn onto the wall surface. The wall is covered in areas of about 900 sq. cms. (a square foot) at a time, with tile cement, into which the mosaic pieces are placed one by one. The cement has to be put on in such a way as to enable the drawing to be followed accurately.

Mosaics made up off-site.

Lay a drawing the actual size of the mural on a floor or table and put the mosaic tiles on it, covering the drawing completely and leaving gaps of 1 to 2 mm. between the tiles. The tiles can be cut with 'mosaic nippers', each one 'nipped' half-way along the intended line of cut. They can be cut and shaped to produce triangles, circles and curves down to a fraction of the size of the basic tile. When the image is complete, glued paper is laid over the tiles, and when this has dried, the paper can be cut up into suitable sections, each of which is numbered, to identify its place in the whole design, and transported to the site. Try to get the best adhesion you can between paper and mosaics when gluing them and be careful how you handle the prepared sections when the glue has dried because they tend to break loose, especially if the tiles vary in depth. Having to replace them is frustrating and time consuming.

Locations for the various sections of the mural will have been drawn up and numbered on the wall. As each mosaic section comes to be put in place, that area of wall is prepared with mosaic cement and the section is pressed onto it. When the cement is dry, the paper or cloth is rinsed off with water.

An alternative method is to use a mosaic jig to make up the mural from your design. These jigs are foot square trays of plastic with indentations to take the mosaics. You put your jig over your design drawing, and by looking through you can copy it into mosaic by putting tiles into the indentations. When the jig is full the tiles are transferred using gummed paper as in method two. The advantages of using the jig are that the gaps between tiles are ideal, that laying up the mosaics is easier. Prepared, foot-square, gummed sheets are available for transferring the mosaics, which make this task, as well as adhering the mosaics to the wall much simpler.

When erecting a mosaic constructed using jigs, the squares will be numbered, cross-referenced with a grid division of the design. It is usual to put the mosaic up working from bottom up and from right to left, a row at a time. The glued paper is removed once a few rows have been put up allowing any tesserae that have moved to be realigned. In both cases the mosaic can then be grouted, and when dry any excess cement on the surface can be removed with dilute spirits of salts, or cleaned off with wire wool.

Mosaic set in cement panels

The mural in this case is made up of mosaic-covered panels bolted or set into a wall. The panels are formed in shallow trays 75mm. deep and up to 700mm. long and wide. The floor and sides of the trays are greased so that the concrete can be subsequently released. The mosaic elements are laid on the floor of the tray, they will at this stage form an image in reverse, and concrete is poured over them, filling the tray. The concrete should be tamped well down and a reinforcement of chicken wire is recommended. Metal fixing rods can also be

Mosaic mural by the Garnet Hill Project Team, directed by John Kraska.

inserted so that the panel can be attached to the wall.

A modification of this method is to use pre-cast paving slabs, bedding the mosaics in 5 cm. deep mosaic cement spread on the surface. Again, the mosaics can be either placed on individually or prepared previously and set out on gummed paper.

Mosaic cement

There are several brands of mosaic cement available. Use a white cement to enhance the mosaic's colours. Manufacturers will advise on which of their cements is most suitable for the job. Look particularly at how long the cement remains usable after first mixing and see if special conditions of surface are required for its use, and if it is sufficiently weatherproof for your location. At present we use 'Ardurit X7' white powder together with 'Ardion 90', an additive which increases adhesion.

Ray Walker, Promised Land - Playground of The Abyss, 1979/80, London.

Freeform Arts Trust, Hoardings around Jubilee Piazza, Covent Garden, 1985.

Chalk and Grime: Into The Future With A Strong Community, 1986, Leith, Edinburgh.

Gilberto Guzman, 1979, Holborn, London.

Ray Walker, Anna walker, Mike Jones, The Hackney Peace Carnival March, 1983/84, Hackney, London.

23

Usually the cement is spread to a depth of one eighth of an inch. Apply the cement with a toothed spreader with teeth about one eighth of an inch apart, one eighth wide and a quarter inch deep. Ensure the mosaic cement is well mixed. Don't make the mix too liquid or the mosaics will slide down the wall, the texture of a heavy cake mixture takes mosaics well, and 'goes off' most rapidly. Grouting is done when the tile cement has sufficiently dried. For this we use 'Ardex C2'.

Each time a small area has been clad in mosaics, clean off the surface with a sponge to remove traces of cement. If the cement is left to dry, such is its tenacity, it will take hours of work to remove. When a large area has been completed it may be cleaned with dilute spirits of salts (subsequently washed off with water) to remove the last traces of cement from the surface of the tiles.

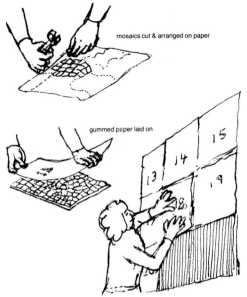

mosaics cut & arranged on paper

gummed paper laid on

mosaics pressed into place on a cemented section of wall

Costs

Costs of mosaic tiles vary according to type and colour, from about £2 per square foot for pastel colours, to £6 for exotic ones.

Colour charts and price lists can be obtained from:

Domus Tiles, 266 Brompton Rd. SW3 2AS. Tel: 071 924 2556.

D.W. & G. Heath. 212A Addington Rd.; Selsdon Croydon CR2 8LD. Tel: 081 657 6349.

Edgar Udney & Co. Bondway, Vauxhall, London SW8 1SQ. Tel: 071 735 2821.

Both the latter supply nippers, grouters, trowels and mosaic cement (which can also be obtained from ceramic tile shops.)

There are many other types of tile cement and grout widely available costing together about £7 for enough to fix 3 square metres of mosaic.

Ceramic Tiles

Britain has a long tradition of tilemaking. Tiles offer textures from grainy matt to highly glazed, and a wide variety of colours. Provided they are fired to a high enough temperature they will last indefinitely. Tiles, being cladding material and produced as identical shaped units, have a natural affinity with the fabric of a building. Their component quality enables them to be used either as pure pattern or images created by artist or group, or as individual elements brought together as a collage. You can buy ready coloured tiles from many manufacturers and stockists in the UK. Smaller tiles can be assembled and put onto glued paper and put up in the same way as mosaics. Larger ones are put up tile by tile. They can also be cut along straight lines.

In this mural by John Watson at Milton Keynes , he pricked out the design with a pastry wheel through a tracing of the full design, onto the claytiles before biscuit firing. After firing the outline, a tiny valley in the clay defined a clear edge for the on-glaze colours, which were then fired. His more recent murals were made using commercial tiles on which the image was painted in underglaze colours, subsequently sprayed with transparent glaze and refired. Where tiles are put up externally, ensure that their water absorbtion is not above 3%.

Clay tiles by infants directed by Tina Gould at Charles Lamb School, Islington, London

Making your own tiles.

Start from basic earthenware clay, wedging, rolling and cutting tiles sufficient for your job, noting that a 30 cm. tile shrinks to 28 cm. after firing. The tiles can be coloured with underglaze (1 to 2 parts) and china clay (8 to 9 parts) slip before biscuit firing, with underglaze and water before glaze firing. Tiles do not have to be of uniform depths, you can raise, dig, carve, model, and add bits to the tiles. They can be fixed to walls by pressing them into a surface mortar render, by pressing them into a tile cement or an expoxy cement or resin.

Alternatively you can start with ready fired tiles and overglaze them. After preparing a full scale cartoon for the mural, draw out the image onto the tiles, work out what colours are to be used, and number and store the tiles until each is ready to be glazed and fired.

Concrete

Blocks

The optimum size for concrete blocks is about 2 foot square, and 2 to 3 inches deep, the size of a paving slab, sufficient to be self-supporting and reasonably light. The slabs can be used as a base for mosaic or for a variety of other materials: tiles, shells, glass, pottery fragments, metal, objects trouvees. Pebbles gathered from various parts of the country give colour contrast. This technique has been used by Philippa Threfall in a number of murals in England.

First the design is made, and drawn up to full scale on paper. Matt or glazed tiles are prepared, and fired, and the natural elements are collected. The blocks are cast with ties or cramps in the back to tie them to an existing wall, the scored front surface is boxed, coated with 'Unibond' and an inch of mortar render is added. The design is divided into sections, and the elements for each section are pressed into the mortar. For increased adhesion they should be coated on the back with 'Unibond'. The advantage of making the image positive, rather than in reverse and pouring from the back, is that you have a greater, more immediate control over the materials and the development of the overall design. After three days the blocks can be released from their frames, cleaned and grouted where necessary and fixed to the wall. The 'unit' construction of the image can be reinforced by contrasting the colour of the mortar between the blocks with that of the blocks themselves.

Concrete Relief

Relief has been used for murals in all cultures, and in the last twenty years concrete has been a widely used medium. There are four methods.

Concrete poured in situ, as part of structure

In this case moulds are attached to the

Bridge in Glenrothes, cast in situ from polystyrene moulds. Created by David Harding.

formwork of the wall, column etc. Some structures are reinforced concrete in which reinforcing steel rods run through the cavity, at a recommended distance not less than 40 mm. from the sides to prevent

rusting. The moulds must be prepared and attached to the formwork before it is erected. In the case of mass concrete, it is sometimes possible to set up the moulds by getting into the cavity after the formwork is positioned.

Concrete poured in situ, as cladding to structure

Here, the wall is prepared by cleaning and removing loose material and by having reinforcing material, e. g. expanded metal or mesh, fixed to it. The mould, on its formwork, is attached to it, the wall is wetted, and the concrete poured in.

Pre-cast concrete

The relief is prepared as a series of panels, so that the weight of the work does not become a problem and so that elements can be independently fixed. The panels can be whatever size is convenient, but if they are to be shifted manually, then 5000 cubic cms. is a maximum size. The panels are made in shallow trays with a base of plywood, with a wooden frame nailed to it.

The mould is placed in the tray and the concrete mix poured in. If the relief is deep or has potentially fragile elements, reinforcing mesh may need to be inserted into the mix.

Concrete modelled on site

Mix an aggregate-less concrete to a fairly dry mix, adding a plasticiser like Unibond, which will help the concrete to stick to the supports and retain any modelled forms. The concrete needs to be supported with expanded metal or chicken wire and

possibly free-standing reinforcement bars. Complicated or detailed effects are difficult to achieve, but consider this method used in conjunction with cast elements, found objects and the like.

Moulds

Traditionally moulds are made of plaster, often cast from a clay 'positive'. When casting concrete directly from plaster, first wet the plaster. It will release naturally but leaves a bloom. To reduce bloom and get a better release, coat the plaster with three coats of shellac, three of wax and one of oil. Expanded polystyrene, because it is so light and easy to cut, is the most frequently used waste mould material, it is also easier to attach to formwork, but remember it must be worked 'in negative'. Polyester resin, plastic and rubber moulds are also used, particularly where repeat castings are required. The best releasing

agents for these are emulsified natural oils. N.B. Polystyrene gives off toxic fumes when cut with a hot wire, so either wear a mask or cut it with a sharp blade.

Mixes

Concrete is made by mixing cement with aggregate and/or washed sand, and subsequently adding sufficient water to dampen all the elements and make a sufficiently malleable mixture to penetrate into all the spaces of the mould and formwork. Prescriptions for the grades and quantities of the elements vary from job to job, and from expert to expert. Generally the ratio of cement to other dry elements will be about one to five. Aggregate size rises with the scale of the work 9 mm. is standard. Concrete takes twenty eight days to cure i.e. to attain optimum strength, although after three or four days it is hard enough for moulds to be removed. Where the mould contains fine details use a 'fatty' mix of concrete, one where there is more fine-washed sand and cement than usual. The mix becomes more malleable with the addition of a little plasticiser like washing-up liquid, whilst Unibond plasticises and strengthens. N.B. When too much water is added the concrete is weakened, also, concrete should not be made in temperatures below 6°C. After pouring, protect it from frost, dry weather, and children (all of which crack it) by covering it with sacking or polythene for a few days.

Vibrating

After the mould has been poured the concrete needs to be vibrated or tamped (beaten). On large works this will be done by contractors with special equipment, but on small ones it is simply necessary to agitate or beat the surface of the concrete until it has been worked into all the crevices of the mould, producing a smooth surface with a watery residue on it.

Cement Fondu

For casting off-site, particularly where the detail is fine and you want strong lightweight panels to attach to the wall, Cement Fondu is used, either in its normal grey state or white (a variety known as Secar 250, which is a good base for colourants). Fondu sets in four hours and cures in twenty-four, during which time it must be kept damp.

While some Fondu panels have been made simply of glass-fibre and slurry, the usual process is as follows. The mould is painted with Fondu slurry, followed by a standard mix of two parts cement, four parts washed fine sand and one of water This is followed by a coat of 'Cemfill' glass-fibre, dipped in slurry and compacted down. Repeat the standard mix and the fibre/slurry layer until the panel is sufficiently thick.

Colouring

Probably the best colouring agents are iron oxides which offer colours from black to marigold to rust. Other agents tend to produce colours which fade rapidly. Colourants should not exceed 10% of the cement, and should be used with a white cement to make them effective.

We anticipate there will be a resurgence of painted reliefs over the next decade, now that there are materials which offer a good lifespan. Artists are looking forward to exploring the possibility of using mineral paints and of applying mosaic to concrete surfaces.

Sequieros working on the metal relief Poly Forum Mural, Mexico City.

Metal

We have already discussed using coach paint and signwriters enamel paint on metal. The following systems are tougher and longer lasting.

Enamel

The technique involves putting glazes onto sheets of steel and firing them. Some artists work on their own panels using their own kilns, others work at or with industrial enamelling firms. Escol Panels of Wellingborough have assisted many artists with the processes and were involved in producing panels for the Tyne and Wear Metro.

Both individual artists and commercial workers are enthusiastic for the system, keen to explore and exploit the nature of the medium and not just use it as decoration e.g. using silk screening to produce images, or to flatly reproduce paintings. Textures and colours in enamelling can be astonishing, the range is limitless. The surface is tough, much stronger than paint, and the colours are fast. The range of finishes varies between a textured, painterly quality to glazes similar to watercolour washes. Costs vary and are difficult to prescribe. Commercial costs depend upon:

1. The number of firings your panels require. Three are obligatory: primer, titanium white and colour firings. If you want to add further glazes, the further firings will cost you more.

2. The cost of panels, which increases according to the amount of preparation that goes into their shape and fixtures.

To get an estimate from an enamelling factory you should send them a specification of panel sizes, numbers and their fixings and an indication of design and colour. An area representative will assist you to work out the specifications and price it.

Escols gave us an approximate cost of £100 per square metre, at the time of writing, for an enamelled work to be carried out.

Cellulose

An alternative method used by Graham Crowley for his Chandlers Ford library mural is aluminium. After finishing, drilling and counter-sinking, the metal is given an etch primer, is sprayed with cellulose colours and dried rapidly under lamps. This system, identical to that used for cars, produces a finish that is very hard and easy to clean, and if British Standard colours are used can be reproduced accurately should they be required for retouching any damage.

Steve McNulty's enamel mural in Central Station, Newcastle Metro.

Moveable Murals

Moveable panels are usually painted on plywood panels, light metal or plastic, and used in a variety of situations: in connection with campaigns or exhibitions which move from place to place; where a wall is available only temporarily or where the surface is unstable or heavily pitted; and where preparation and painting are better done off-site. Some commercial clients may stipulate a preference for a mural being painted onto panels rather than directly onto the wall, as the wall may mask service conduits or they may require the option of replacing the mural in the future. In some cases it is not possible to get direct access to the wall because of building work etc. so working off site is the only option. The use of panels also allows a greater flexibility of working schedules, painting during the winter or in the evenings for example, and may allow you more time to complete the project. It also enables people to participate who prefer to work on ground level and indoors and with all the benefits of a studio space.

Fixing the panels to a wall is usually done by first screwing or rawl-bolting lengths of timber (e.g. 2 inches x 1 inches) to the wall, then screwing the panels to these. We emphasise that panels, whether wooden or metal, in external or damp conditions must be protected on all surfaces, back, front and edges with an impervious layer of oil-based paint. Fixing temporary structures is best achieved by screwing through the mural to free-standing timber structures or by bolting through to clips on scaffolding.

Hoardings

Most development sites are surrounded by plywood fences to mask the

Lubiana Himid and Simone Alexander: portable anti-racism mural.

activities within and protect pedestrians without. It used to be the fashion to inolve schoolchildren in the design and painting of hoardings to improve their appearance, and many fine ones were produced in the 1970's.

Freeform were among the first to see the real potential for artists here, and their lead has been followed by several artists and groups. This is the most 'commercial' application of public art, whilst rewards are often high, competition is intense. Developers are increasingly cost conscious and it is

Freeform Arts Trust, 'The Great Fire', Development site hoardings iin the City of London.

not unknown for undercutting to occur. There is as well a need to encourage developers to maintain their enthusiasm for enhancing the environment as well as their desire for advertising themselves.

Hoarding murals are usually made up of 8 foot by 4 foot plywood sheets nailed to timber frameworks or suspended from scaffolding. Since a hoarding's life may be anything between six months and three years there is a need to consider what quality the ply should be, and what type and quality of primer, paint and varnish to use, relative to its expected life-apan, the brief and budget.

Since hoardings are transient they offer opportunities for arty experiment on a grand scale, and some developers have welcomed the theatrical and witty designs which characterise the genre. Existing hoardings have included, besides straight painting, fretworked overlays and shaped panels. Artists have explored and integrated cutaway viewing niches, pedestrian walkways, fake people and all sorts of spatial illusion and reflection. Nylon reinforced vinyl scaffolding sheets have also been decorated, and some designs on them have been executed through a computer aided painting system.

27

Contracts

COMMISSION AGREEMENT

THIS AGREEMENT is made
the .... day of .... 19 .... between
(NAME) ....
(ADDRESS)....................................
(TELEPHONE) ....("the Artist") and
(NAME) ....
(ADDRESS)....................................
(TELEPHONE)...................("the Commissioner")
by which we agree as follows:

1. COMMISSION:
The artist agrees to create on or about the . . . day
of........... 19 .... the following proposed work of art ("the
Work"):
(DESCRIPTION)..
....
DIMENSIONS) ....
(MATERIALS) ....

2. PAYMENTS:
(a) In consideration for creating the Work the Commissioner agrees to pay the Artist the sum of £ . . .
(excluding V.A.T.) in the following instalments:
(1) One third upon signing this Agreement and
(2) One third when the Artist notifies the Commissioner
that the Work is approximately two-thirds completed
and
(3) 0ne third when the Artist notifies the Commissioner
that the Work is completed. For these purposes, the
Artist shall notify the commissioner in writing and shall
permit him/her or his/her authorised agents, upon
giving reasonable notice, to inspect the Work.
(b) Subject to Clause 7 of this Agreement, the Artist
shall retain title of the Work, and all rights therein, until
payment of the final instalment.

3. ACCEPTANCE:
It is understood that the Artist will use his/her aesthetic
skill and judgement to create the Work, and the Commissioner agrees to accept the complete Work unless
he/she can show that the Work was not executed
substantially in accordance with Ihe description agreed
by him/her under Clause 1 of this Agreement.

4. ACCESS:
If the work is to be created on site, the Commissioner
shall arrange for the Artist and his/her authorised
agents to have access at all reasonable times to the
site between the.......day of........................ 19 ....
and the.......day of........................ 19 ....

5. DELIVERY:
(a).Unless the Work is to be created on site, the *Artist/
Commissioner- shall arrange for delivery of the completed Work to the site on or about the   ....day
of...........................19.........
(b) The costs of delivery (including packaging, transport, and insurance) shall be paid by the Artist/Com-
missioner.*

6. SALE:
Upon completion of the Work if created on site or upon
delivery of the completed Work, both parties shall sign
the Contract of Sale (see 'Artists Contract of Sale'
right).

7. TERMINATION:
The Commissioner may terminate this Agreement at
any time upon giving written notice to the Artist, who
shall be entitled to receive or retain payment for all
work done in pursuance of this Agreement up to date
of receiving such notice. In the event of termination,
title to the Work and all rights therein, shall be retained
by the *Artist Commissioner.'

8. PROPER LAW:
This Agreement shall be governed by the law of
England and Wales and may only be amended in
writing by both parties.

9. ARBITRATION :
Any dispute under or arising out of the Agreement shall
be referred to an arbitrator, nominated in accordance
with the provisions of the Arbitration Act 1950 or any
Statutory modification or re-enactment thereof for the
`time being in force.
(SIGNED)
(The Commissioner) ....
(The Artist) ....

COMMISSIONED DESIGN AGREEMENT

THIS AGREEMENT is made
the .... day of .... 19 .... between
(NAME) ....
(ADDRESS) ....
(TELEPHONE)........................... ("the Artist") and
(NAME) ....
(ADDRESS) ....
(TELEPHONE)......................("the Commissioner")
by which we agree as follows:

1. SUBMISSION OF DESIGNS:
The artist agrees to submit ......design(s)/model(s)
/maquette(s)/sketch(es) on or about the...... day
 of ....19 ..., for the following proposed work
of art ("the Work"):
(DESCRIPTION) ....
....
(DIMENSIONS) ....
(MATERIALS) ....

2. APPROVAL:
The Commissioner shall, within.........days after the
submission of the design(s) notify the Artist of his/her
approval of the design(s) and his/her intention to
proceed with the Work.

3. CHANGES:
If requested in writing by the Commissioner, the Artist
agrees to submit up to.......additional designs for the
Work.

4. FEES:
The Commissioner shall upon signing this Agreement
pay the Artist a design fee of £.............
If requesting any additional designs under Clause 3 of
this Agreement, the Commissioner shall pay the Artist
an additional design fee of £...................... per design.
Fees do not include V.A.T.

5. COPYRIGHT:
Subject to Clause 7 of this Agreement, copyright in all
designs for the Work is *retained by the Artist/assigned
to the Commissioner.

6. COMMISSION:
If the Commissioner notifies the Artist of his/her intention to proceed with the Work, both parties agree to
sign the Commission Agreement (a copy of which is
attached hereto).

7. TERMINATION::
If the Commissioner does not no-
tify the Artist of his/her intention to proceed with the
Work, the Artist shall be entitled to retain all design fees
payable under Clause 4 of this Agreement. In the event
of termination, title to the design, and all rights therein,
shall be *retained by the Artist/assigned to the Commissioner.

8. PROPER LAW:
This Agreement shall be governed by the law of
England and Wales.
(SIGNED)
(The Commissioner..
(The Artist)...

* Delete whichever does not apply.

ARTIST'S CONTRACT OF SALE

Date:...
Place of Sale:..
Title of Work:..
Description of Work: medium ....
               dimensions...........................
               size of edition.......................
Sold to: name ....
       address...
Artist: name..
       address ....
Price: £.................
Terms of payment:
The words and figures set out above describe the date
the place, the purchase price and the terms of payment
of this contract of sale of the above mentioned art work
However, in order to protect the future existence and
use of the work, the parties further mutually agree as
follows

1. ORIGINALITY :
The artist hereby convenants that the work is his/her
original and that he/she shall not produce a replica o
it.

2. EDITION:
If the work is one of an edition (as stated above), the
artist hereby covenants that the size of edition shall no
be increased after the date of execution of this contract.

3. REPRODUCTION :
Although the copyright in the work is retained by the
artist, the buyer shall be entitled to permit the reproduc-
tion of the work in books, art magazines and exhibition
catalogues.

4. CARE OF THE WORK:
For as long as the buyer owns work, the buyer hereby
covenants not intentionally to alter, damage or destroy
the work.

5. RESTORATION:
If the work is damaged, the buyer shall notify the artist
and give the artist a reasonable opportunity to conduct
or supervise, the restoration of the work.

6. ARTIST'S EXHIBITION:
The buyer shall lend the Work to the artist once in every
twelve months for a maxim period of six weeks for the
purpose of inclusion in a public exhibition of the artist's
works, if the artist gives the buyer reasonable written
notice of his intention to do so together with documen-
tary evidence of insurance cover and prepaid carriage
to and from the exhibition; provided that the artist
ensures that the exhibiting institution identifies the
work as belonging to the buyer.

7. PLACEMENT OF WORK:
If the buyer places the work with any person or institution for exhibition, re-sale, or any other purpose, the
buyer shall immediately write to the artist stating where
the work is placed.

8. ADDRESSES:
Artist and buyer shall notify each other in writing
immediately of any change in address.
(SIGNED)
(Buyer)...
(*Artist/Artist's Agent)...

SUGGESTED MODIFICATIONS

The following modifications to these forms are suggested as a result of their use in the West Midlands:
• **Commissioned Design Agreement**
9. PUBLIC LIABILITY
If the artist is to spend some time on site researching
content of a design it may be necessary for him/her
to take out Public Liability Insurance even during the
design period.
• **Commission Agreement**
2. PAYMENTS
It is recommended that the second payment is made
when the work is half completed, not two-thirds
completed; this is because it is may be difficult to tell
much difference between a work two-thirds complete and quite complete. Indeed a work of art often
gathers momentum in the closing stages so that the
two-third completion stage may be reached quite
late in a project.
4. ACCESS
It is useful to insert a clause that the artist will not be
responsible for delays caused by the commissioner
not having the site ready for access, execution and/
or installation of the work. (e.g.: If the wall is not
ready for the mural it is not the artist's fault. We have
heard of one case where the wall was not even built
at the start of a contract!)
6. SALE
This can be omitted for simplicity, but according to
Henry Lydiate, unless there is such a clause the work
will always belong to the artist.

Reprinted by courtesy of Henry Lydiate, Steve Field and Tim Ostler.